Do Your Lessons L[
Students?

MW01044646

Strengthen your culturally responsive teaching by designing curricula that leads to equitable, humanized outcomes. In this powerful new book, Jessa Brie Moreno and Mariah Rankine-Landers reveal how artistic research and creative inquiry across subject areas and grades can help you access your learners' collective wisdom and potential. Moreno and Rankine-Landers describe the SPIRAL framework for centering culturally responsive teaching and learning through the arts, showing how and why these iterative processes lead to liberatory outcomes.

You'll learn how to use creative inquiry to address power dynamics in teaching and learning, and how to critically reflect on your curriculum, including investigating whose narratives are centered, whose have been erased, and which marginalized stories can be brought forward. You'll also find out how to alter the learning space to set a container for creative practice, which is key to navigating cultural shifts, building trust, and setting a collaborative and collective mindset.

The book offers a variety of practical activities you can implement right away, such as using visual art making, writing, and storytelling as prompts to activate meaning making and to disrupt unconscious biases, as well as using creative dialogue and character development for embodied learning, introspection, and identification. With the addition of this book to your professional library, you'll have new tools for building belonging and justice, and engaging all students through artistic research, dialogue, and deep listening.

Mariah Rankine-Landers (she/her), M.Ed., and **Jessa Brie Moreno** (she/her), MFA, founders and co-executive directors of Studio Pathways, have each been liberatory educators and artists for over twenty years, having collectively taught at the pre-K through post-graduate levels. They are sought after professional facilitators who work with educational and executive leaders, and teachers leading for social change. They are co-creators of *Rise Up: An American Curriculum* and have co-designed creative pedagogy for The Othering and Belonging Institute out of UC Berkeley, The Center for Cultural Power, and the WKKF Foundation (Racial Healing). They are former co-directors of the School Transformation Through the Arts and Integrated

Learning Specialist Program out of the Alameda County Office of Education. Partners include NAEA, The Kennedy Center, Stanford University, Museum of the African Diaspora, and many county offices of education, school districts, individual schools, arts organizations, and philanthropic and social change institutions. Follow them on social media platforms at @StudioPathways and at studiopathways.org.

Do Your Lessons Love Your Students?

Creative Education for Social Change

Mariah Rankine-Landers and Jessa Brie Moreno

Routledge
Taylor & Francis Group

NEW YORK AND LONDON

Designed cover image: Adia Millett, Gravity, 2022 Acrylic on wood panel
36 × 48 in | 91.4 × 121.9 cm

First published 2024
by Routledge
605 Third Avenue, New York, NY 10158

and by Routledge
4 Park Square, Milton Park, Abingdon, Oxon, OX14 4RN

Routledge is an imprint of the Taylor & Francis Group, an informa business

ISBN: 978-1-032-29354-7 (hbk)
ISBN: 978-1-032-24897-4 (pbk)
ISBN: 978-1-003-30122-6 (ebk)

DOI: 10.4324/9781003301226

Typeset in Palatino
by SPi Technologies India Pvt Ltd (Straive)

Dedication

We dedicate this book to Zaretta Hammond, our mentor and friend in shaping the thinking of Do Your Lessons Love Your Students? *Her work has built a new foundation on which to make the profound connections between the brain, culture, and the visual and performing arts in education. Zaretta, we are ever grateful for your mentorship and care.*

Contents

Foreword

Foreword by Julie Kendig
Director of Inquiry, RISE Research & Evaluation, United States.

The arts provide a way to honor, recognize, and uplift the gifts of culture that our students bring. Studio Pathways' process and learning engagements have allowed educators to open doors for students in ways they may not have felt the permission or the comfortability with before. We have been partnering with Studio Pathways to research and understand the influence that their frameworks, approach, and pedagogy have on educators and leaders.

The data revealed significant changes in the everyday practices of educators. Through in-depth interviews we learned about profound transformations of those whose eyes were opened to the unintended challenges they had been perpetuating for learners who live in bodies of culture. We saw relief among teachers and leaders of color who have been struggling in educational spaces to place equity and antiracism at the center of the conversation. Studio Pathways' methodology, based in a culture of care, allowed space for varying viewpoints. In their professional development sessions, Studio Pathways modeled what is possible in classroom spaces, and teachers walked away from their sessions feeling joyful and encouraged, wherever they were on their journey to becoming culturally responsive. Time and again interviewees shared how using Studio Pathways' practices helped them slow down so that they could introduce care and sensitivity to students' lineages, cultures, and personal needs. This didn't just create deeper relationships among the students and teachers, it also allowed students to flourish holistically.

As educators learn to create opportunities in the classroom and curriculum for the space to be smudged with connection and belonging, there is an expansive opening in the imagination and a mindset shift of what is possible in education. Focusing on the gifts each "radiant child" brings, trusting that students' lineages and lived experiences are the roots from which freedom and creativity will grow, using connecting practices and rituals regularly–these are all ways to nourish young hearts, minds and bodies and show care for one another. This work is so beautiful, and I am deeply grateful to have played a part in it.

Acknowledgements: Lineage of Love

Mariah would like to lovingly acknowledge: My grandmother Mary, and my mother Gina, Jojo, Jesse Floren, Jerry Sharp, Nikosha Orchard, Joe Mutow, Mia Birdsong, Yvette Murrell, Nicole Boucher, Dr. David Hemphill, the Trees, the Rankine clan, YOU, my students, families and colleagues from Shelby School, Capitol Montessori, PS7, and NOCCS. Special thanks to Dr. Giuseppe Ciaravino and Alessandro Thompson.

Jessa is ever grateful for: My grandmother Letitia, my mother Lisa Reinertson, Sierra, K. Lily, Paloma Chiara, Johnny Moreno, Jack Ruszel, All My Loving Family both Given and Chosen, The Aunties and the Cousins, Ena Dallas, Jaisri Dixon, Tamara Sabella, Lera Boroditsky, Taylor Pedersen, Christopher Struitt, Alex Craven, My Glorious Teachers, Judy Bock, Antonio Fava, Doniel "Sotz" Soto, Linda Lowry, Albert Takazaukas, Pamela Eakins, Anne Bluethenthal, Kris Brandenburger, Monique LeSarre, Cindy Shearer The Bay Area Theater Community, OakTechRep, OTAI WCCS, USC, CIIS, SJSU, Dina Watanabe, Charlene Meyers-Sponholtz, Thery Jenkins, Vita Hewitt, Lauren Gerig, Lorraine Sela, the Flag Team, a vast lineage of (especially female/femme) writers, artists, and thinkers where my soul has found resonance, and Emmylou.

Together we would like to acknowledge: NOCCS, STTARTS, ILSP, Susan Wolf, Constance Moore, A'aron Heard, Maya Kosover, Derek Fenner, Tongo Eisen-Martin, bell hooks, Sir Ken Robinson, Maxine Greene, Norma Wong, Cannupa Hanska Luger, Kerry James Marshall, Hank Willis Thomas, Julio Salgado, Amy Sherald, Julie Kendig, Julie Kuwabara, Jah Yee Woo, Marvin K. White, Charlotte Saenez, Diane Friedlander, Miko Lee, Lily Jones, Carolyn Gramstorff, Amy Robinson, Janet Heller, Jennifer Mineer, Jahan Khalighi, Sofia Fojas, Margie Chardiet, Perla Yasmeen Melendez, Marilyn Zoller Koral, Elizabeth Rubenstein, Carrie Wilson, Geoff Vu, Andy West, Stacey Wyatt, Jane Lee, Carolyn Carr, Lily Janiak, Sujin Lee, the Inflexion Team and The Weavers, john a powell, Roxanne Dunbar-Ortiz, Yvette Jackson, Brett Cook, Tana Johnson, Chip McNeal, Todd Elkin, Arzu Mistry, Indi McCasey, Dominique Enriquez, Brooke Toczylowski, Rebecca Osiris Prather, Maria Laws, Lois Hetland, Julia Marshall, Louise Music, Shakti Butler, Jeannie Russell, Unique Holland, Sarah Crowell, Evan Bissell, Colette Cann, Anna Deavere Smith, Mary Stone Hanley, Demetri Broxton, (T)sedey Gebreyes, Kati Silva, Anna Maria Luera, Kat Evasco, James Kass, Marc Bamuthi Joseph,

Jeff Chang, Favianna Rodriquez, Michelle "Mush" Lee, Jessica Mele, Delia Reid, June Wilson, Caitlin Brune, Diana Cohn, Tom Corwin, Jeremey Sugerman, David Shulman, Melanie Graziano, Christy Tran, Dr. Jose Morales, Teddy Zmrhal, Alphabet Rockers, Destiny Arts Center, Agency by Design, In Cahoots Artist Residency, Houser & Wirth, the Jack Shainman Gallery, the Panta Rhea Foundation, the Stuart Foundation, The Laird Norton Family Foundation, the Robert Wood Johnson Foundation, the Hewlett Foundation, The Center for Cultural Power, Yerba Buena Center for the Arts, Museum of African Diaspora, The Kennedy Center, Turnaround Arts, Stanford Live, The Othering and Belonging Institute, and with special thanks to Adia Millett.

Indigenous Land Acknowledgement

We remember that all non-Native people to this land are settler occupiers, many brought against their or our will. Studio Pathways acknowledges the Ohlone people of this land that we live and work on. We pay our respects to their people, their elders, past, present and future, and recognize that sovereignty was never ceded—it was never given up. We also acknowledge the continued legacy of systemic racism stemming from the historic inequities of genocide and enslavement that equally require a process of truth and reconciliation in our nation. This acknowledgement is but a first step toward taking action to rematriate Indigenous land and recenter Indigenous cultural ways of being.

Figure 0.1 Mirror Shield Project, by Cannupa Hanska Luger.   Action on November 18, 2016, at Oceti Sakowin Camp, Standing Rock, North Dakota

Origin Story

Mariah Rankine Landers and Jessa Brie Moreno are the *we* of this book. We come to this work as practitioners who understand the need for an overdue reframing of the narrative and purpose of education, work that is often theoretically spoken of, yet seldom actualized. We are teachers, artists, creators, mothers, aunties, community stewards, and good friends. We come from rich cultures of experience in classroom teaching, rigorous arts disciplines with extended traditions, and single mothers who were teachers and artists themselves in towns in the Central Valley of California. Our brains were wired through the study of cultural anthropology, dance, the land, theatrical and fine arts, integral studies, interdisciplinary arts, and equity and social justice in education. We share similar schooling experiences from our time in the California K–12 public education system. We are situated in mixed race families, across borders, cultures, and generational pursuits of justice, arts, and education. Between us we have taught pre-K to post-graduate students, taught special education, coached leaders across sectors, and implemented artful pedagogy through lessons that love. As a Black bodied woman and a white bodied woman, we have found resonance in our shared leadership as a way to model and hold creative processes for social change.

We first met as educators and artists in Oakland, California, and collaborated a decade later, during four years of collective leadership for School Transformation Through the Arts, or STTARTS, a U.S. Department of Education Grant. Working with two middle schools in East Oakland, we situated arts, culture, and creativity as central forces for learning. This work expanded arts integration to address equity issues, racial injustices, and ethical dilemmas found in schools deemed failing by standardized metrics. The teachers and staff in these schools were working to educate their students in the face of trauma-inducing socioeconomic circumstances rooted in oppressive systems.

With a thoughtful team of creative coaches and administrative support, bold transformative teaching theory and practices were introduced and sustained. Although both schools faced controversial closures soon after, caregiver participation increased, teachers designed units of instruction centering arts that increased engagement and learning outcomes, and in-school detention spaces became restorative arts-based rooms. These closures acted as wind on dandelion seeds, as numerous educators who participated in this work went on to inhabit positions of leadership in educational and organizational capacities, disseminating the power of culture and creativity in learning environments. Others took up creative practice full time, shifting their internal identities from teachers who make art to artists who educate.

In these years, alongside our leadership with the esteemed community that was the Integrated Learning Specialists' Program, we identified an arc of learning that wove together our lived liberatory understandings of teaching, pedagogy, artistic experience, and justice. Studio Pathways was born.

> What I have seen in newer learners to this work is that it's not about the structure—we're gonna do a land acknowledgement and then we're gonna look at an artwork and then we're gonna ... etc. It's about a mindset shift. Do your lessons love your students? Once we get the mindset shift, then we can do the practice and we can go deeper into the inquiry of "Who do you want to be in this world?" and "What do we want to practice?" For new learners this can be uncomfortable, but if you value this you'll do it anyway, and you'll stop yourself when you're not in alignment with your values. We all get off base sometimes. But can we reset? Can we recognize that we need to step back and ask ourselves "Is this how I want to show up?" and "Is this what I want for the world?"
>
> –Anna Maria Luera, Director of Artist Leadership,
> The Center for Cultural Power

Research Methodology

In the development of this book, we engaged with Julie Kendig and her RISE Research and Evaluation team, who originally partnered with us through the STTARTS program at the school sites we once served. Julie, through her invaluable insight as an Indigenous-identified researcher on James Catterall's team with Centers for Research on Creativity, became an ongoing partner in the elusive work of developing qualitative research on creativity in educational practice. Over the next several years, she developed a series of inquiries around the implementation of our frameworks with our partners. Her research questions included the esoteric, such as "How can we understand the way forward within learning contexts, which are made up of complex and sometimes conflicting worldviews, cultures, and epistemologies?" and the pragmatic, including, "What does this practice look like in real life?"

Like any creative act, it is intended that the concepts presented in this book will continue to evolve and expand in your hands. We hope it will help you bring clarity toward the social change needed in the schools and organizations you lead, the classes you facilitate, and the students you cherish. We invite you to:

◆ Process information through the arts experiences we've mapped out, which are designed to support an unfolding of knowledge as unique as each fingerprint on the planet.

◆ Stay in collaboration with others throughout the process of engaging with this text.

◆ Work in ongoing cohort-centered learning, or "communities of practice" as an ideal form for practicing the methods and pedagogy shared throughout this book.

◆ Collaborate with local artists, activists, and community arts organizations; collaborate with the flexible curricular frames, and most importantly; collaborate with the learners you love as creative beings themselves.

Part One
Art as Love

Part One:

Art as Love

Figure P1.1 Graphic image depiction of Part One: Art as Love.

SPIRAL Logo designed by John Ruszel. © Studio Pathways, LLC.

1

A Pedagogy of Love

Figure 1.1 A photograph of a school window at Alliance Middle School, Oakland, CA. 2015. The word love printed in bold letters across the window.

Photograph by author.

DOI: 10.4324/9781003301226-2

What do we mean when we use the word love? Love in education is a verb, an action being called forth on the path to a creative and liberatory teaching and learning stance. Love illuminates the components, motives, and complexities of this path and moves us forward into a pedagogical shift in current educational practice. To arrive at an experience of joy and well-being in learning for learning's sake requires a nuanced understanding of love in action.

The role of love in teaching and learning can be activated by asking the question, "Do my lessons love my students?", an inquiry that compels us to do the work of acknowledging and understanding a history of education that has not always loved our humanity. Pause and consider what love in education means in our current global and local contexts. Love might mean acknowledging and understanding that a core purpose of education in this precarious time is how to grow our inner selves and collectively evolve.

Do Your Lessons Love Your Students? is an invitation and provocation for teachers and leaders across educational contexts to sit with our pedagogy, our teaching methods, our procedures, and the curriculum we teach. It serves as a throughline to develop the knowledge, wisdom, and capacity to be a love-based teacher. We know firsthand how hard it can be to focus on big picture theories when you are teaching, grading, navigating multiple subjects, meeting caregiver and administrative demands, and supporting many young minds with distinct needs. It may feel hard to know, let alone love, your students, your lessons, or even your chosen profession.

> There is definitely a love-based something going on at Roots. That is probably the most powerful thing at Roots. You can't define or measure what love is. They try to understand and dissect it. No philosopher, scientist, statistician has figured it out. There is something brave about the fact that they teach from their hearts and out of love. It's tangible in the ways students talk about and relate to and show love to their teachers.
>
> – Jane Lee, Educator

There's a Place for Love in Education

Teaching itself is a great leap of faith and a great act of love. To believe in someone's capacity for growth and to see their inner radiance is love. To understand the critical role teachers play in shaping the future, and to personally commit to pursuing teaching as a calling, is also love.

Do Your Lessons Love Your Students? is a vision for a just and creatively inspired society. It is a guidepost for social imagination pointing us toward vibrant schools where children expand their creative and critical thought. It is a call to action to remove the violations on the human spirit and rigid conditions that are currently ingrained in much of schooling. It is a gentle nudge to recreate systems, structures, policies, curricula, lessons, and methodologies.

Educational philosopher Maxine Greene (1995) was an early advocate of the role of social imagination in creating social change. Without a social imagination, we may fall into ingrained beliefs and patterns and carry out dull expectations for what's ahead. Aligning our thinking toward a brighter vision involves taking actions to repair a past that has not served us and invoking methodologies that will activate creative potential in our children.

When a caterpillar goes through metamorphosis, the contents of its body liquify and become a soft mass. It is the role of the imaginal cells that survive the disintegration process to grow into the form required to make a butterfly a butterfly. At first, imaginal cells are seen as threatening to the caterpillar, but eventually the butterfly emerges. Many agree that there is currently a necessary disintegration of much of what education has been before. What is the potential for education if we participate as imaginal cells do?

Movement practitioner and Zen teacher Norma Wong teaches her audiences to practice envisioning the brightest story. From the brightest story of the future that we can imagine, it becomes possible to map the actions and goals to arrive at the places we conjure in our creative mind. We share in a social imagination that the field of education can shed old systems and prioritize liberatory pedagogy, centering the arts as a pathway where our students will step into the brightest story.

Do Your Lessons Love Your Students? invites you on a path of both theory and practice, what can also be called *praxis*, as you connect the dots between culture, cognition, and the role of creativity and the arts in education. It is a journey in which you will hopefully see yourself reflected and acknowledged, in the expectation that your teaching practice will help our society to remove any remaining barriers to a liberatory experience of learning and of life.

Recently we sat with elders and leaders from a group who participated in the conceptual development of wraparound services, now practiced nationally. These social service workers show up as love-based practitioners with a consistency and persistence which spans decades. Love in this organization supports youth through services from the time they start school into adulthood. What stands out about this kind of love is that even when a relationship is hard, they still show up. When there is resistance, they still show up, because they have a shared vision for people having lives that are worthy of being well lived. They are the embodiment of what a removal of barriers looks like, or love in practice.

Teaching as Sacred

Throughout history, the role of the teacher in society has been a revered and even sacred position. Mentorship and apprenticeship have been rooted in two primary relationships: the relationship to the lineage of knowledge sets, and the relationship that flows from mentor to teacher to student and back again. Education that is siloed, overly focused on content standards and test-based outcomes, on depositing knowledge rather than drawing it out, or what Paulo Friere (1970) referred to as the banking method of education, has not gotten us to stronger outcomes as a society and planet. Any knowledge set devoid of context and meaning and relationship is incomplete. Likewise, a caring relationship alone does not constitute a purposeful and compelling curriculum.

In reviving a humanistic purpose of the role of education, we stay with the concept of love as a guiding force. Through the lens of love we examine the success of our lessons, our classrooms, our policies, and our institutions. Lessons that love our students extend into how well the culture and contexts we live in love our students. Lessons that love our students contain an implicit or explicit ethical stance that prioritizes the interconnectedness of all beings.

Designing lessons rooted in a love ethic requires digging into our shared histories, unearthing complicated stories of the self and of our lineages, and sometimes dissecting social power structures and narratives. In this process we may find ourselves sitting with other human beings, people with evolving inner selves on their own complex and nuanced developmental paths, struggling to achieve a sense of beloved community. Firmly planting our teaching practice in a core human concept like love, we become better equipped to understand and empathize with each other's stories, perspectives, and experiences. We are far from the first to propose a pedagogy of love as a way forward, but we are in a long line of good company in the pursuit of dynamically changing how education is practiced. Let it be evident to the future that we choose love as the guidepost for course correcting a system long overdue for a rehaul.

A Thinking Protocol for Love

Designing from a stance of love means a reevaluation of practices, strategies, and methods. Development of the LOVE protocol came from a need for assessments to evolve alongside the ethical understanding of a love-based pedagogy. The LOVE protocol is an example of how we might look at our learning outcomes not through the lens of right and wrong, but instead through the actual meanings they hold for us. Thinking protocols, also known as thinking routines, are mechanisms that can help us to specify discrete observations, connect and bridge ideas, and form insights through critical reflection. They encourage "thinking about thinking." Thinking protocols and routines can be used flexibly by the instructor in place of formative or summative assessments and with students as self-assessment, as peer-assessment, and as a whole group process. They often take the form of memorable acronyms, verbs, or alliteration to make them accessible processes to recall from memory.

The LOVE Protocol

Select a focal point on which to practice this protocol, wherever you are right now. Perhaps you've selected a song that's playing, or a poem you have memorized, or a work of visual art a student or child gave to you. Ask yourself:

- ◆ Love: What do you *love* about this work, art piece, project, film, etc.?
  - O Start with this question to allow the mind to focus on what is meaningful to you as an observer. What compels, resonates, and what is there to be appreciated? Starting with love is an asset-based approach to critique, reflection, assessment, and evaluation processes.
- ◆ Observe: What do you *observe* about this creation, artwork, experiment, etc.?
  - O Observe closely and notice any details, choices, and processes present in the piece. Use your senses and prior knowledge to help your mind make connections as more knowledge is attained.
- ◆ Value: What do you *value* about this work, art, experience, experiment, etc.?
  - O Weigh in on what is worthy of appreciation, allowing your mind to determine what is meaningful within the context of your own knowledge, aesthetics, lived experiences, or belief systems. Add significance to the subject at hand.
- ◆ Evolve/Expand: What might you *expand* upon or see *evolving* from this work, art, experience, experiment, etc.?
  - O Consider what might come next from this piece. Imagine and evaluate ideas, claims, or things that might be missing from the current state or condition of the work. Evolution and expansion encourages us to understand that creative processes and learning outcomes can be lifelong. There is often tension as an

artist in knowing when a piece of work is done. Developing an awareness of when a piece is complete enough over time comes through continued reflection and evaluation.

Before you read on, we invite you to use the LOVE protocol to consider a lesson you love to teach. What do you love about this lesson? What do you observe your students doing and making connections to when this lesson is taught? What do you value most about this lesson? What can you continue to expand upon and how might you evolve it?

L.O.V.E.

WHAT DO YOU LOVE ABOUT …

WHAT DO YOU OBSERVE ABOUT..

WHAT DO YOU VALUE ABOUT…

WHAT CAN YOU EXPAND OR EVOLVE ABOUT…

Figure 1.2 The Love Protocol.

Bibliography

Contra Costa Youth Services. (n.d.). https://wccysb.org/

Friere, P. (1970). *Pedagogy of the Oppressed*. Continuum Publishing Corporation.

Greene, M. (2000). *Releasing the Imagination: Essays on Education, the Arts, and Social Change*. Jossey-Bass.

Lee, J. (2019a). Interview by M. R. Landers.

Lee, M. (2019b). "Mush." Presentation to STTARTS Cohort.

Wong, N. (n.d.). https://resonance-network.org/workshopping-the-world view/

2

Creative Process for Social Change

Figure 2.1 "Owl/Heart" by Susan Wolf, 2016.

Mixed media collage.

DOI: 10.4324/9781003301226-3

In 2006, Sir Ken Robinson posed the essential question, "Do schools kill creativity?" and sparked what continues to be the largest viewership for a TED talk in history. In his talk, and in his life's work to promote creativity across sectors, he proposed that we all have a vested interest in education because we all care about the future. He went on to make a convincing case that creativity is the learning outcome *most needed* in schools today, which is our viewpoint and in many ways the premise of the book before you.

What if schools did not kill creativity but nurtured it? We pose to you the not-so-outrageous idea that for schools to be truly creative spaces they must love our children by providing lessons that love our students. In order to determine if lessons love our students, we need to ask if our schools love our children. To know more, we'll need to reach mindfully into our past to reckon and repair, analyze the stories about learning that have shaped us and continue to influence our thinking, and identify harmful power structures and replace them with those that are more liberatory. In doing so, frameworks like culturally responsive teaching and learning through the arts may start to become a more obvious way forward.

If you ask someone to describe a time they were taught something of value, people will often immediately go to a story of a grandmother or a cousin or an early childhood teacher. They will locate someone who took the time to see them for who they were, who imparted a skill or understanding needed to advance in that moment. The lessons and learning that we remember most often tend to be coupled with compelling emotional or sensory experiences. Sometimes these are feelings of care or empathy, other times of curiosity, discovery or excitement, and other times of trust, discomfort, and risk.

Memorable teachings are often held within our cultural ways of knowing, through making or creating something, such as a quilt or a dumpling. On the surface these lessons may have been teaching us a skill, but they were usually situated within a larger frame of *deep culture*, a concept that we first encountered through the work of Zaretta Hammond in her book *Culturally Responsive Teaching and the Brain* (2014). *Deep culture* is where our belief systems, values, and ethics come into play. Quilting might be a way to teach us the value of keeping a loved one warm or repurposing fabric scraps as resources. Learning to cook and host a delicious meal for others from a recipe that has been passed down imparts a value system of hospitality, care, and generosity. Science now backs up the idea that care in learning is cognitively sound and that tending carefully to learning contexts and relationships helps the brain to learn (Jackson, 2014).

A roomful of principals and superintendents sat listening to Yvette Jackson, the keynote speaker, adjunct professor at Columbia University, describe why relationships and learning environments are key priorities for culturally relevant teaching. She showed us several images of neurons and described the myelin sheath as the fatty substance that grows fatter when the brain and body are in a safe learning environment. Yvette went on to describe that when learners are in distress and trauma takes place, the myelin sheath breaks down, making knowledge acquisition sometimes impossible. She spoke about the ways we might reframe the Gifted and Talented Programs to understand that all children are gifted. She spoke on the ways that education needs to center methods on supporting learners to cultivate high quality intellectual thinking ... where abstract thought was key to the equation. I thought about a prior student who one day started throwing chairs around the room. It was me, 20 five-year-olds and a child who was taking out rage on everyone. I wrapped my arms around the child and scooped him up. I held him tightly as I was trained to do for emotional outbursts. I called the office for support, but no one was available. I told my students to line up, and we all walked together to the office. I told my class we need to get Bumi the support he needs. In the days that followed I rearranged table seating, brought in bean bags, and created a corner that was less jarring than the previous set-up. This was a classroom with no windows, so I brought in a lamp from home to make the lighting less obtrusive. I made incremental changes to the schedule increasing rest, play, and art in a school that demanded scripted ELA, phonics, and math curriculum. I traded out blasé plastic manipulative for songs, dance and many creative acts of learning. By the end of that year Bumi's mom walked in, hugged me, and said, thank you for changing my son's life. Thinking back, I credit my interventions to a curriculum that did not love my students in responsive ways and a grueling school day that lacked joy, towards a love-focused and artfully attuned environment that changed the lives of all my students that year.

– Mariah

So much of the work of lessons that love our students rests on how well we understand the science of trauma and acknowledge that every human experiences pain. It is heartbreaking, of course, to witness a child exhibit adverse childhood effects, but there is power in knowing that we can create conditions that will nurture them while in our care.

In the United States, public education is still mostly based on an industrial-age understanding of the world, developed far prior to the massive influx of information available through technology today. As swiftly as our technology has advanced, our educational system has become outdated. One of the most outdated and harmful aspects of our U.S. educational system is that it was constructed to provide either distinct pathways or roadblocks to those aspirational notions of *life, liberty, and the pursuit of happiness*. The quality of our educational experience has mostly been dependent on our position in society, or what author and historian Isabel Wilkerson (2020) refers to as the U.S. caste system. Our racialized identities, our perceived genders, our socio-economic status, our abilities, and our first languages are a few of the factors that compartmentalize us, moving us along a predetermined track toward or away from academic achievement. This established ranking of people based primarily on racial categorization is why we prioritize reckoning and reconciliation.

> It is the worn grooves of comforting routines and unthinking expectations, patterns of a social order that have been in place for so long that it looks like the natural order of things.
> – Isabel Wilkerson, *Caste: The Origins of Our Discontents* (p. 70)

If we look together at the relic that still stands as schooling today, it becomes clear that new educational approaches are necessary. Shifting course toward theories and practices driven by creative processes will create the social changes we desire. It will also be important to understand the role of culture in the development of this level of transformative educational change. Despite some overwhelming circumstances, it is an exceptionally powerful time to be an educator. While the structures that have held up our institutional educational systems are cracking apart under the weight of inequity, pandemics, and subpar learning and working conditions, in their place new paradigms are springing up.

Liberatory theories are being met with the contemporary practice of hip-hop pedagogy. A culturally responsive approach to teaching is being connected with evolving understandings of cognitive science and our socio-emotional intelligence. Cultural wisdom is being reclaimed by mentors, educators, and elders of all stripes. Caregivers are reimagining their role in education and folding into the fabric of community school models. Schools across public, charter, and private spheres are connecting with Indigenous leaders and land justice efforts. Ancient technologies are accompanying new ones as teachers and organizational partners at individual school sites include the natural environment, land stewardship, and the creation of new media arts into and beyond the standardized curriculum. These sustained efforts at transformation are promising and hopeful.

Just as we no longer have time to wait on addressing climate change, we can't wait for another generation to create loving, creative schools. Throughout this book we travel from the "what and why" of educational change and into the heart of "how to".

> Sitting next to the great teacher of teachers Dr. Sonia Neito is a memory one does not forget. At the dinner table were local educators and a few education funders. As we discussed the state of education and spoke about the role of teaching through the arts, we all noted the power of creativity in teacher practice. Thoughts were shared on the outcomes of integrated teaching practices based in learning through the arts. I remember Sonia responding that the work of teaching the mind to think critically and creatively was "just good teaching." The phrase has stuck with me as a motto of sorts.
>
> – Mariah

What Is the Relationship Between Creative Process and Social Change?

Creativity is the act of combining ideas to create something new. Some might say that creativity is innovation, an aha moment, or a phenomenon. Others might understand creativity as only belonging to those who inhabit a certain category of inherent genius. It is our belief that humans are inherently creative beings with the capacity to create far beyond our perceived limitations. Is creativity a viable pathway to liberated thinking and being?

Creativity can be considered the capacity to follow and fuse ideas and thoughts, allowing new forms and conceptual thinking to emerge. For quite a long time, psychologists and researchers have given consideration to two core qualities of thinking that seem to comprise creativity; divergent and convergent thought (Bruno, 2007).

Figure 2.2 Divergent and convergent thinking.

Divergent thinking is considered primary in developing our creative ability to think outside a narrow scope of possibilities. This is where we generate and come up with multiple and varied big ideas. Divergent thinking can take us from believing, for example, that we can only use an object for its intended purpose and into conceiving of an array of uses for that same object. It takes us from a single story about a person, place, or thing to intersectional understanding and multidimensional conceptualization. Divergent thinking can help us to reimagine a basket as a lampshade or imbue a rock formation with human facial features.

Convergent thinking allows us to make choices and take action around our divergent thoughts. It is the process of thinking through how things fit together. It allows us to combine and merge and distill ideas to create something new and novel. Divergent thinking relies on convergent thinking in order to help us decide on creative action. Convergent thinking helps us to select the tools and resources at hand that might bring our creativity to life.

Our creative actions are also activated within our unique cultural contexts, and these contexts can either serve to constrain or free our creativity. Every thinker has cultural orientations informed by the environment, values, knowledge sets, customs, languages, and cosmologies of the cultures they are a part of. Creative impulses change our realities, and creativity changes culture.

Why does this matter for our schools? There are many ways to define creativity across cultural contexts. In co-development of the School Transformation Through the Arts rubric with the team from Centers for Research on Creativity, we were concerned that looking for evidence of divergent thinking might not always be the best measure, especially if it is not experienced as a cultural asset to be divergent. For example, cultural arts often place a high value on perfecting practices passed down through oral traditions, embodied techniques, and direct lineages of a craft. In these spaces, creativity might look like repeating the same series of actions with accuracy in order to become more expert in a skill set handed down through apprenticeship.

A young female-identified student from a nondominant cultural group and low socioeconomic background may not "score highly" on divergent thinking rubrics involving decontextualized imagination, but can improvise innovative healthy meals for her siblings from limited resources day after day. A culture bearer running a community arts center that keeps a traditional dance form alive may not be applying divergence to the art form directly, but is certainly using both divergent and convergent thinking to keep a specific cultural practice available to future generations. A transgender student may use fashion and makeup in creative ways as an external divergent talisman to signify convergence with an internal identity others may not recognize.

Contemporary artists, while often mentored in lineages that require convergent thinking, often apply both divergent and convergent thought to the act of innovative creation. When we remember to contextualize creativity within culture, a lot of human creativity can be seen as the result of an imaginative response to the conditions we experience.

> We were driving past a shop in west Jamaica. My grandfather, noting the plastic on the ground said, "When I was a yout we used a 'stan at di shop and getta drink. But you know what di drink was in? A clay cup! We would grab drink and smash di cup on di ground." He took his hand and made a gesture of smashing something on the earth. I reveled in his memory of Jamaica in the 1930s and took joy in thinking about this sustainable creative way of producing and using resources. This cultural practice was a creative action in direct relationship to the environment itself.
>
> – Mariah

Our environments and even our own interests will serve to limit or expand our creative actions. Which clay, or discarded plastic, is available? What design will we replicate because it suits our needs or appeals to our aesthetics? How do the cultural contexts and the environment of our schools limit or expand creative thought and action for our students and ourselves? Try using both divergent and convergent creative thinking in the design of your lessons. What might our lessons look like if we allow ourselves to think in divergent and convergent ways about our lesson design and teaching practice?

Curriculum as Creative Act

Most of us find joy in self-expression, whether it is recognized as creativity or not. Simple acts such as hair and clothing choices, gardening, decorating our homes, even dancing at a wedding are all avenues to express a seed of the creative impulse within us. As educators, lesson planning can likewise—don't laugh—become a joyous artful act. This may sound absurd from your current perspective, or maybe you already found a creative spark in your lesson development, which is why you've picked up this book.

> The year that I got my teaching credential was the year the *No Child Left Behind* (NCLB, 2001) policy was implemented. I remember feeling dismayed as I read through the newly adopted standards. I got into teaching because I remembered the classrooms my mom taught in. She would have students create nearly life-size representations of whales and ocean animals and hang them from the ceiling for her Ocean unit. That is the kind of teaching I was expecting to do. Instead, I spent my student teaching in a classroom where the lead teacher spent the entire morning on math and the entire afternoon on English Language Arts, reading from a script. It was painfully boring to sit there day after day and then try to emulate a policy-based style of teaching that was an affront to students and me.
>
> Instead of selecting a public school to teach at once I got my credential, I opted for a Montessori school where creativity was encouraged. However, it brought its own set of issues, and highly racialized ones. I then moved to a school with a 98 percent Black student population and fell in love with the community; however, I was back in a setting where NCLB policies dictated what and how I taught. Determined to lead with integrity, I found divergent ways to teach the new set of standards, which often meant redesigning canned curriculum to be more responsive. I relied on integrating the arts into everything I did. My room was nicknamed "the action room" by the principal. This was not necessarily a compliment. I did not have permission

and proceeded anyway, in my conviction for creating learning conditions that were engaging, bright, joyful and love-filled. My students excelled. I am still in touch with many of them to this day. It wasn't until I moved geographies and started teaching at an arts integration school that my creative curriculum design was valued.

– Mariah

Figure 2.3 The arts are how we get to everything.

Cultural and Contemporary Art in Creative Practice

Creativity is intrinsic, and a birthright.

– Liz Lerman

When educators are asked to identify an artistic practice, a common response can be "Oh, I don't have one. None. I'm not an artist. I only cook. I only make dolls. I only make this (phenomenal) craft or dance this (incredible) dance from my culture. I'm not an artist." There are an abundance of creative acts that humans engage with on a regular basis, however the idea abides that if it's not signed and put on a museum wall, it's not art. We'd like to disrupt that mythology and entertain a new mythology, one that imagines that we all are artists, and that as artists we are capable of transforming reality.

By invoking an artistic identity, one that applies our unique creative talents and curiosities, we can be of greater service as teachers. Prioritizing creativity in our classroom practice can be a portal opening out to a vista of the social change potentially available to us.

So when teachers claim that they don't have a creative bone in their body, we push them, just a bit, to reconsider. Usually there is a memory attached to the moment they decided they were not a "real" artist, a time they were shamed for not drawing a straight enough line, or were unable to replicate an accurate feature, or hit the right note, and in that moment they gave up on artistic practice. Some of us compare our own creative abilities to other people's, which falsely validates a sense that we are not creative. It's simply not true. Teaching is an inherently creative process. It demands creative thought to plan out a day, teach content, and care for a community of learners. There is a lot to be gained from making these creative practices more intentional.

Sometimes the witnessing of our students' creative spirits can be the impetus that inspires us to move just beyond our comfort zone and serve better through opportunities to make art. Where we might be unskilled or unpracticed, our students will often surprise us by excelling. Any visit to a museum or gallery will remind us that art is not always about perfecting the features of a face or accurately depicting the colors of a sunset. There is a misconception that creating perfect replicas is the goal of arts practice, but contemporary artists use technique and skill to illuminate concepts through creative expression. Creative techniques, like any other subject area, can be cultivated through extended practice. The more you practice creativity, the more creative you will be.

Any act that is cultivated by a practiced application of the forms and principles of that discipline through divergent and convergent thinking may be called an art. Cultural arts practiced in the home or the life of the community are often overlooked. Because these creative practices are usually held by women or female-identified folks, they have been relegated to the category of "craft" and considered inferior in the art world. Tragically, craftspeople themselves often dismiss the value of their own creative practices.

Despite the overwhelming mythology, cultural arts are indeed art, and contemporary artists are usually not isolated geniuses. They are often innovating off of a lineage attached to a particular cultural arts practice. Contemporary artists evolve their work from the artists that came before them. They meld techniques they may have apprenticed in or played around with into the talent and experience they bring as creative individuals. Our cultural arts lineages may place a high value on the study and replication of what has come before in order to carry traditional knowledge forward. Contemporary artists look to expand, evolve, or combine that historic knowledge with self-expression. This can be seen in work from contemporary artists such as Faith Ringold, who famously combines the rich lineage of African American female quilting with current social commentary, or in the artistry of Cannupa Hanska Luger, whose *Future Ancestral Technologies* combine traditional and commercial Native Arts lineages with contemporary contexts and a view for complicating the narrative around indigeneity (2021).

As an important sidenote, all artistic lineages can and should be considered cultural arts, as they were born of a particular set of cultural realities, aesthetics, and norms. Works once called "classic" because they were constructed and canonized within a European or North American worldview can be looked at as cultural artifacts or traditional rhythms or tribal mythologies like any other.

One teacher working with us startled themselves when they realized that their otherwise solid visual arts curriculum contained only culturally European or North American works of art and only white-bodied, male-identified artists. This was not at all representative of the cultural lineages or gender identities found within their student population. Rather than staying stuck in a place of personal shame or defensiveness in this self-discovery, this teacher set out to diversify the representation of the art and artists they referenced, but wanted to keep the same themes and curriculum, which they felt were working just fine. In a year's time, they had completely reworked their curriculum to contain 100 percent contemporary artists of diverse identities and cultural backgrounds connected to the students in their classes. What was even more surprising was that their approach to instruction had also completely changed, and they had begun treating students as artists coming to their own studio. The teacher provided access to materials, resources, prompts, techniques, guidance, and living artist exemplars, but otherwise the time was now given over to the students to create. This teacher had found their own giddy sense of liberation at being a "guide on the side" for the flourishing artistic community they had nurtured into being.

Bibliography

Alameda County Office of Education Integrated Learning Specialists' Department. (2014). STTArts: USDOE grant. https://www2.ed.gov/programs/artsedmodel/2014/alameda.pdf

Bruno, F. J. (2007). *Psychology: A Self-Teaching Guide*, John Wiley & Sons.

"Change the story/change the world: Episode 64—A conversation with Liz Lerman—change the story/change the world." (2023, February 1). Captivate.Fm. https://change-the-story-chan.captivate.fm/episode/episode-64-a-conversation-with-liz-lerman-ch-2

Greene, M. (2001). *Variations on a blue guitar: The Lincoln Center institute lectures on aesthetic education*. Teachers' College Press.

Hammond, Z. (2014, November 13). *Culturally Responsive Teaching and the Brain: Promoting Authentic Engagement and Rigor Among Culturally and Linguistically Diverse Students*. Corwin Press.

Jackson, Y. (2014). *Pedagogy of Confidence*. Teachers College Press.

Kendig, J. (2022). *RISE Research and Evaluation: Studio Pathways Qualitative Research Outcomes*.

Luger, C. H. (2021, January 1). *Future Ancestral Technologies*. Ayin Press. https://ayinpress.org/future-ancestral-technologies/

Nieto, S. (Ed.). (2005). *Why We Teach*. Teachers' College Press.

No Child Left Behind. (2001). http://www2.ed.gov. https://www2.ed.gov/nclb/landing.jhtml

Ringold, F. (1996). *The Sunflower Quilting Bee at Arles*.

Robinson, S. K. (2006). Do schools kill creativity? TED Talk.

Wilkerson, I. (2020). *Caste: The Origins of Our Discontents*. Random House.

Part Two
The SPIRAL Framework

Part Two:

The SPIRAL Framework

Figure P2.1 Title page. Part Two: The SPIRAL Framework.

3

The SPIRAL Framework

A Practical Frame for Liberatory Learning

Figure 3.1 A dedication for love centered change.

DOI: 10.4324/9781003301226-5

The spiral is an apt metaphor to hold the applied pedagogy of culturally responsive teaching and learning through the arts, due to its central and expansive place in an unfolding universe.

Fun facts:

◆ The spiral is the shape of our galaxy and the shape of the majority of known galaxies in the universe.
◆ Spirals are repeated throughout our living systems, from the double helix of our DNA to the swirl of a new leaf or shell.
◆ Spiral representations have been found symbolically across cultures and are central to multiple human cosmologies.

Figure 3.2 Snail shell. Turnart Collection @gettysignature.

Evoking a spiral image as a metaphorical framework for liberatory learning can help us reinforce the understanding that knowledge is an ever-evolving process. It expands and unfolds and can be seen as iterative in nature, both returning to center and broadening in scope. Galactic spirals, for example, are not fixed forms, but nevertheless they have stability. For us, spirals are a metaphorical reminder that we are always in process of growth and that our task is a continual return to love.

The SPIRAL Framework contains elemental concepts that comprise what we call culturally responsive teaching and learning through the arts. It has been designed to fluidly and flexibly support and coincide with many cognitively sound frameworks educators already use such as Universal Design for Learning, Teaching for Understanding, Understanding by Design, and Experiential Learning. It guides intentional choice making towards an antioppressive, antiracist, anticaste educational structure, with regard for the whole child, the whole school, and the whole community.

Figure 3.3 SPIRAL Framework.

We're not just trying to teach subjects, but we're teaching people, human beings, young people, who have trauma and triumphs, ancestry and rich knowings and experiences.

– Jahan Khalighi, Director of Programs, Chapter 510

Bibliography

Kolb, D. A. (2014). *Experiential learning: Experience as the source of learning and development* (2nd ed.). Pearson FT Press.

Nemeth, K. N., & Brillante, P. (2017). *Universal design for learning in the early childhood classroom: Teaching children of all languages, cultures, and abilities, birth–8 years.* Routledge.

Wiske, Martha Stone. (1997). *Teaching for Understanding.* Jossey-Bass.

Wiggins, G. P., & McTighe, J. (2005). *Understanding by Design* (Expanded 2nd ed.). Pearson.

4

The Studio Pathway

Cultivating a Studio Mindset

It's Not a Strategy, It's a Pathway

Strategy
/ˈstradəjē/

The concept of strategy and strategic thought can be traced to militatristic origins, tactics meant to be carried out in battle or in war.

Pathways
/ˈpaTHˌwā/z

Pathways evoke directionality and process, the route one travels in order to arrive. There are both neural pathways and treelined ones.

Figure 4.1 Definition of strategy and pathway.

DOI: 10.4324/9781003301226-6

Often when we work with school sites or organizations, educators plead for culturally responsive strategies to immediately implement, or strategies for achieving arts standards, and we understand these practical requests. Educators want to take action and immediately do things that will integrate the arts and cause less harm. While we know firsthand that applying a thoughtful rubric or employing a particular thinking protocol is a step on the pathway, it is not a holistic solution. If a checklist on its own would transform education, we would implement it! Without an accompanying mindset shift around the purpose and intention of education, and a reevaluation of our ingrained assumptions and biases about how we learn, lasting change cannot be achieved. It turns out that when we tend first and foremost to "a pedagogy of love" through the development of a learning environment that nurtures creative thought, the result is an authentic culture shift.

Just as science has radically altered how we understand physiology and nutrition in the past few decades, so neuroscience has begun to change our collective understanding of education. Federal food guidelines many children and families grew up believing were scientifically optimal for physical health have had equal roots in economics and agricultural policy (Jahns et al., 2018).

Dietary guidelines stand as an appropriate allegory for the current system of public education. Just as a diet low in vitamins and minerals is now seen by much of the scientific community as a culprit in many poor health outcomes, so might we now understand that our public education system was likewise founded on economic imperatives that were not in service of how the brain actually learns. Just as our children deserve nutritious food, our students deserve an education designed to optimize their cognitive capacities.

Why a Studio?

When we talk about a *studio pathway* we are talking about two core ideas and locations. The first is the external, physical learning environment where meaning making takes place, and the second is the internal development of the mind where thinking is nurtured. A *studio pathway* is something we can relate to quite tangibly, reimagining classrooms as actual studio environments intended for acts of creation.

A *studio* is a culturally responsive setting for learners to make meaning, explore, reflect, and evolve their intellect and inner selves. A *studio pathway* is a practice of invoking creative processes that can lead to personal growth and change. When we are in studio practice with others, we are able to advance useful skills for democracy: collaboration, communication, critical thinking, and connection. When we are in studio practice by ourselves, we are in direct relationship with the art form or medium, working with our inner consciousness and growing into new ways of thinking.

When educational philosopher Maxine Greene spoke about the concept of a transmutation of information, she was referring to the ways that the environment supports our mind and body to make interconnected knowledge apparent (2000). Greene asked educators to consider the alertness of thought invoked when we engage learning through the aesthetics of the environment, through the arts, and through creative response.

It is important to remind ourselves that learning extends beyond the classroom. The powerful thing about an artistic mindset is that artists can create art everywhere. Any place can be a studio when an artist wants it to be, so don't lock in the idea that a studio-like setting only takes place indoors. Let's continue to alter current ideas of what a classroom or school can look, be, or feel like.

Classroom as Studio

My introduction to the Studio Habits of Mind was a pivotal moment in my teaching career in 2007. At first they did not make any sense whatsoever, aside from the idea of reflection. But as I explored the role of arts in my teaching, they became a cornerstone of my practice. The Studio Habits of Mind, known as SHOM, codify the habits embodied by artists as they make and create art.

They are, in no particular order: Reflect, Express, Engage and Persist, Stretch and Explore, Understand the Art World, Develop Craft, Envision, and Observe (Hetland et al., 2007).

At Harvard's Project Zero, I deepened my knowledge and practice of the studio habits with colleagues Todd Elkin and Arzu Mistry. I remember feeling more confident about practicing the studio habits because I was witnessing their impact from a Brown-bodied teacher, Arzu, and heard her success stories in both East Oakland and India, where she was using the habits to teach children in settings where it was believed the arts should not be a priority. I started to consider how I might introduce the habits to my students in a culturally responsive way. With an awareness that theories from an Ivy League school might not be *exactly* culturally relevant, I decided to test them out on myself. I walked through museums and used the studio habits to reflect on the art I was seeing. I can admit to you now that before my introduction to the wider world of arts integration through the Studio Habits of Mind, I really did not have an awareness of the contemporary art world. I had taken art history courses in college, so I knew about Pollock, Picasso, Gauguin, Dali, and Cassat—you know, all the dead white artists. But I didn't have an awareness of the vast exciting world of contemporary arts. I became obsessed with noticing. I became obsessed with learning about artists and what they had to say. Spending more time with art meant becoming a more multidimensional person.

I decided to introduce one habit a week to my students. I made a big colorful wheel and told my students that I wanted them to learn how to think in ways that would help them understand the world. After a month of consistent practice, students could be heard using the language during their play—an authentic assessment that allowed me to understand that they were building comprehension and fluency in these habits of mind. Caregivers would check-in with me in the morning and tell me a story about how their child, who was having some challenges with tying their shoes, shouted, "It's okay—I just have to engage and persist!" Did my heart swoon? It absolutely did.

The Studio Habits became a primary tool that I used to support my students. We even renamed our after-lunch choice time to Stretch and Explore, which shifted expectations of how students spent that time. Students would set an intention about what they were going to explore during this section of the day. I would ask them, "How did you stretch your brain today?" They would then report back on what they had explored.

This is how I began to change my ideas around the role of the physical classroom. The classroom was more joyous when I thought of it as a studio space. Once this shift happened for me, I started to play with the forms and functions of "stuff" in my classroom. I swapped out individual materials for communal supplies and added more art tools that students could access at any time.

The classroom as a studio took on dimensions of its own. When I had family support, we would often have the back door open so students could go outside to work on more messy projects. When I didn't have caregiver support, I created a system with the classroom sink and a few extra buckets of water where students could manage their art making.

As my classroom became a studio, I relaxed my idea of what students should and could do when they arrived in the morning. Often parents would take a moment with their child before they left and co-create an artistic piece or read a story together. It was touching.

There would be days when I would release the schedule to "make and create" all day. During our rainforest unit, we had a deadline approaching: Exhibition Night! Much like an open house, except students were to show their dynamic learning and knowledge acquisition through performances of understanding. My students created a rainforest experience as they studied the Amazon, with a focus on the interdependence of living things. They each selected a rainforest animal or insect to artistically research while we collectively made the layers of the rainforest, showed how those layers worked together, and represented animals living in the different layers. Students created a dance to signify the role of the mighty strangler fig, which decomposes a living tree and creates a new ecosystem for other plants and animals to live in. They loved learning that a strangler fig grows from the droppings of sloths in the canopy, so they decided to create a six-foot stuffed sloth.

With exhibition night approaching, and my students in a frenzy of excitement to show off what they learned, I needed to provide them with more time to make the elements of the rainforest. Here's what I did with twenty-two five and six year olds: We moved the tables to the sides of the room. We rolled out huge sheets of butcher paper. We were making seven or eight trees each about 6 ft tall. Some of them had to be made in the adjoining hall area. Students worked on them in groups. Due to the gravitas of the trees, students had to first sketch the tree out on scratch paper and agree to how it would look. Because joy is contagious, I taught my students how to champion each other's artwork. If they were done with their contributions they could look for more to contribute or give props to the artist. My classroom would sound like this: "Yeah, Shabira!! That looks amazing!" and "Good Job, Andre!" or "I love it, Rosie!" Music to my ears.

We had several making days like this. They were exhausting but fun! At the end of one of our installation days, also a studio practice,

Alex, a jubilant child, ran up to me and said, "Ms. Landers, Ms. Landers, we forgot one thing! The rain!!!" And in the next swoop he turned to his classmates and said, "We have to make raindrops!" They hurriedly began to make drops of rain out of blue paper. I then called the principal for a ladder because I had not thought of this, and found myself attaching drops of rain hanging from yarn to the ceiling of the classroom.

– Mariah

What if every classroom was composed and choreographed as a studio? What if studio thinking was a guiding principle for developing critical thinking in our students? What if students had the materials and spaces they needed to process and show what they know through meaningful engagement with the world around them?

A Place for Healthy Risk

Missing from the evocative actions articulated by the Studio Habits of Mind is the role of risk, which signifies divergence and is also a component of artistic thinking. Our over-reliance on direct instruction has meant that students have a hard time knowing how or why to take a risk in learning. Educators and social scientists are beginning to advocate for the idea of failure as neutral, or even desirable, rather than devastating. In risk-tasking, students can make attempts and see what works and what doesn't, eliminating the failure debate altogether. In the arts, creators are able to make decisions and take risks to see how things take form and need reshaping, redesigning, or recreation. As educators, we can uplift the notion of healthy risk-taking as a desirable process in both our teaching and students' learning. In the rainforest unit, artistic risk taking allowed for students to trust in their own processes and to gain real knowledge about complex concepts.

The next time you walk into your classroom, imagine it as a studio. What gives it studio-like qualities? What decisions can be made by students? What's missing from your current space in order to physically or aesthetically make it feel more like a studio? Does the environment provide space for students to artistically research the topics at hand?

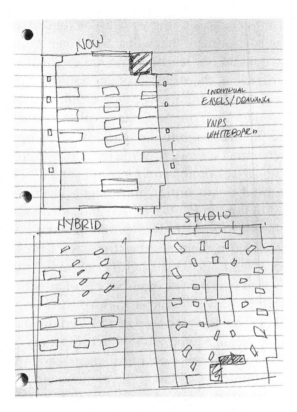

Figure 4.2 Classroom studio concept sketch by a high school math teacher.

Alter and Altar the Space

Altering and "altaring" the space is a way that we can put our attention to the aesthetics of learning. The space where we learn is equally as important as the content we teach. Were you taught that the environment is the third teacher in the classroom? It actually might be more like the first teacher. Our bodies pick up patterns and cues before our brains have the chance to perceive them. Our consciousness extends to the environment around us, and we are connected to the objects, land, and space as one infinite experience. Considering how atoms and electrons behave, it is not irrational to perceive that we are linked to and even defined by what we are surrounded with.

Altering with an "er" and altaring with an "ar" both require creativity and artistry to shape an environment that will support learners. When we *altar* our learning spaces, we invite our learners into the co-creation process. Making an altar where students can share objects of importance, such as photos, drawings, or plants, is a culturally responsive practice. Students feel and gain a sense of belonging when they have opportunities to alter, and altar, the classroom. They build a sense of attachment to the space. When learners feel attached to their space, they construct a sense of pride in their learning. This is different from simply building a welcoming environment. We can all design welcoming classrooms, and should, but including our students in an artful design process can dramatically shift how students feel seen and cared for at school.

In 2014, teachers in the STTARTS program were invited to bring an object of importance with them for the first day of professional development. We cleared a shelf and laid brightly colored cloth on top. Flowers were placed in a vase in the center. A few words of intention were placed on index cards around the flowers. Teachers added their objects of importance to the altar, and it became the way they introduced themselves to the learning group. Each day teachers were invited to bring a new object to place on the altar. Stacey Wyatt, then principal of Alliance Academy, remarked about the loss of altar building in Oakland. She commented that it was once an active practice, particularly in East Oakland public schools. She beamed with awe that the community had returned to this form of sharing, intent, and respect for learners. Altaring with an "ar" can shift the feel of a room. It can heighten the senses and reshape a classroom space from feeling institutional to feeling connected with purpose.

When artists set up their studios, be they in a rehearsal hall or field or closet or living room, they often intentionally consider how to design a container that will support a transformative process. They might consider how much light is needed, how much space is needed, what materials and protections from the elements are required, what music to listen to. How many of us consider our classrooms as a container that can likewise support transformative creative processes? We spend so much of our lives in these settings. Is your classroom setting a place you look forward to spending time in yourself? Tending to the aesthetics of space is a way to tend to creative thinking and well-being.

As teachers, often at great expense and personal cost, we already engage in setting up our classrooms each fall, but the script we follow in classroom set up often results in an all too predictable arrangement and aesthetics. Altering with an "er" allows us to play with shapes, configurations, and the needs of learners. When we alter as an artist might, with a studio in mind, we can change the form and function of a classroom.

Educator A'aron Heard gave their class the signal. They held up their hand to make the symbol of a quiet coyote. With a timer in their other hand, they counted down, 3, 2, 1 … I watched as students shoved items away in backpacks and pushed their desks from group configurations into one large U shape around the perimeter of the classroom. "You did it! 1 minute, 19 seconds! Give yourself a pat on the back!" Their sixth graders grinned and then stood ready for the next set of instructions. A'aron had been practicing to rearrange the classroom from one studio setup to another studio setup. In the first iteration, students worked in small groups. In the second, students needed space to activate theater processes. Did I mention this was middle school? And they only had 50 minutes for each class session? I was transfixed. A'aron was accomplishing what seemed impossible. Their students were eager to switch settings because it signaled the next learning session. Students went on to use the new open space to share dialogue as they crafted scenes connecting to the history content they were learning.

– Mariah

While the theater arts are ensconced in ritual, and most performing arts classes could be considered altered/altared spaces in many senses of the word, I did not experience actual altar-making practice in a classroom until I co-taught with Dr. Monique LeSarre. The undergraduate integral studies program we taught in was cohort-based, and learning took place over several long weekends. Learners in the space were often returning to complete an undergraduate degree after a long absence from academia in order to pursue and experience life beyond the walls of a classroom. Dr. LeSarre would arrive early before class with items from nature, flowers, and dry foodstuffs such as rice and beans, in addition to her lesson plans.

As a Black, biracial identified therapist, Dr. LeSarre would create beautiful mandalas, or circular patterns, at the center of the room, carrying out this practice as an extension of rituals rooted in the African diasporic experience. These would remain as a focal point throughout our classroom practice, with students adding to this altar over the course of our weekends together, bringing in their own cultural items from home and flowers, notes, and sketches from the classroom experience in real time.

By creating a fixed intention point meant to reflect beauty and bring elements of nature to the experience of learning, Dr. LeSarre was reviving a practice that has been in place in cultures around the world. It is recognized that some organized religions prohibit the use of altar making for spiritual purposes in public practice, in which case we believe that altering space with an "er" can be a creative alternative. The nature-based mandalas Dr. LeSarre created intentionally brought a sense of the sacred to the experience of teaching and learning, which was appropriate for the context of our classroom study. Focused on objects of beauty, rather than on the professor in front of the room, there was a felt sense of an intentional collaborative learning environment.

Final presentation weekends in this learning cohort could be quite long, as each student shared oral reports embodying their personal experience and lessons from the course of the semester. It stretched one's ability to listen, so Dr. LeSarre made this a shared mandala making time, so that listeners could engage in a physical act while being an attentive audience. The quality of listening became more thoughtful, reflective, and mindful. Simultaneously, we brought forward the idea of a "love note," a way of sharing back with the presenter the words, phrases, and concepts we had loved hearing.

Each presenter would receive a multitude of love notes after they shared their work, which was often the most poignant feedback. Some of the male-identified students in particular named that it was a point of disruption and narrative reframe to give and receive love instead of engaging in critique or competition. Students reflected that the experience of being seen and heard by their peers was far more meaningful for them than what we as teachers named in our more formal written assessments and rubrics.

I have been moved to see more schools and organizations take up the practice of nature-based mandala making and assessments through love notes and to see the extended community practice of altering/altaring space. These are humanizing rituals that inspire classroom practice. In fact, during the challenging school closures that faced Oakland a few years back, one of the schools we had worked with created a collaborative, nature-based mandala to alter/altar space as a form of activism on the school's front steps. I'm grateful to have been mentored in this love-based practice, and to be a part of the lineage that has returned the concept of altering/altaring educational space to classroom settings.

– Jessa

Figure 4.3 Mandala image. Flowers, beans, and natural objects arranged as an altar during professional development.

Bibliography

Greene, M. (2000). *Releasing the Imagination: Essays on Education, the Arts, and Social Change*. Jossey-Bass.

Seidel, S., Walters, J., Kirby, E., Olff, N., Powell, K., Scripp, L., & Veenema, S. (1997). *Portfolio Practices: Assessing & Thinking Through Children's Work*. National Education Association.

Hetland, L., Winner, E., Veenema, S., & Sheridan, K. M. (2007). *Studio Thinking: The Real Benefits of Visual Arts Education*. Teachers' College Press.

Jahns, L., Davis-Shaw, W., Lichtenstein, A. H., Murphy, S. P., Conrad, Z., & Nielsen, F. (2018). The History and Future of Dietary Guidance in America. *Advances in Nutrition (Bethesda, Md.)*, *9*(2), 136–147. https://doi.org/10.1093/advances/nmx025

5

Creative Inquiry

Learning Through a Creative Pursuit

At the most accomplished levels of any professional pursuit, creative inquiry is alive and well. Physicists, scientists, engineers, psychologists, writers, and artists are often driven by a question with real-world implications to which they apply divergent and convergent thinking. Creative inquiry can be a gift of possibility where learning goals might actually limit potential. Creative inquiry provides students with authentic meaning making, intentionality, and purpose, and builds up their intellective capacities. It expands on background knowledge to include current contexts and values future-facing perspectives. It creates an avenue for successful pursuit of knowledge, as creative inquiry has few wrong answers.

An inquiry-based approach to teaching and learning is something that most educators now have some practice in. Essential questions can be found in many if not most whiteboard configurations these days. Even state and national frameworks have begun to emphasize the role of inquiry. Creative inquiry in particular asks: "How can we come to know things better through a creative pursuit? What questions am I, and the students I serve, genuinely curious about understanding?" Creative inquiry points to but does not prescribe how to arrive at a particular learning outcome. At the end of a study, there are often more questions than answers. This can be a huge reframe.

Replacing learning goals with creative inquiries immediately invites a more complex thinking process to the table. This can feel unwieldy to educators and students used to a model of didactic lessons and yes/no, correct/incorrect binaries. Of course, discrete skills, techniques, and critical thinking

DOI: 10.4324/9781003301226-7

methods will still need practice in order to arrive at that which we call fact. In pursuit of any particular line of thinking or subject matter, there are often many compelling and reasonable outcomes to the same inquiry question.

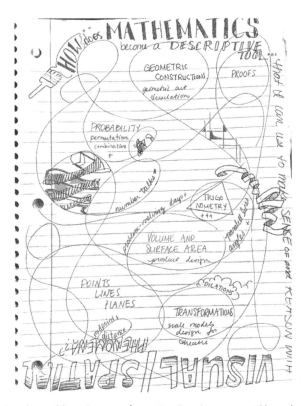

Figure 5.1 Mathematics throughline. Image of creative inquiry process. How does math become a descriptive tool?

Creative inquiry is a process of engaging deliberately with both the known and the unknown during the unfolding of a lesson or unit. Related to, but not to be confused with, more narrow standards, objectives, or goals, creative inquiry builds upon the authentic curiosities of both teacher and learner. Rather than a standardized learning outcome such as "Students will be able to describe the hunter-gatherer societies, including the development of tools and the use of fire," a creative inquiry might initially be reframed as "How did early humans collectively advance their societies?" and upon reflection evolve into "Where do we come from? Where are we going? In what ways have our lives been shaped and impacted by the development of tools and the use of fire?"

As a new educator, I was asked to be culturally responsive by differentiating learning, meaning to create several different lesson options daily for the over one hundred theater and creative writing students I taught. Distinct from accommodations, which I of course provided to students in need, differentiation was a well-meaning but maddening approach, requiring more time than there were hours in a day. I could only fail. When I finally trusted myself to try bringing forward a few key creative inquiries around the themes that resonated loudest in our curriculum, I found that I could spend my time developing a really meaningful question or elegant prompt. My students could apply curiosity and different creative approaches to their thinking, still technically "meeting the standards" and yet coming to their own differentiated conclusions.

– Jessa

Opening up the possibilities of a closed standard or goal through the generative process of creative inquiry allows our students to know more about the subjects at hand and increase meaning making to include a wider range of concepts and ideas connected to the subject. Students move from recounting information without comprehension or analysis into purposeful knowledge. There is no longer a stopping point to the learning, and it's possible to enter from many angles and arrive at many conclusions.

Creative inquiry expands our students' participation in the navigation of their own educational experience. Rather than taking this journey as passengers, students can have an active role in arriving together at a destination no one else has been to in exactly the same way before. Crafting a powerful creative inquiry or set of inquiries provides a nuanced form of indirect instruction. The conclusions each individual arrives at will be distinct based on their own conceptualization and experiences in the world. Inquiry-driven education in general is an active, engaged pursuit of both knowledge and understanding. On unexpected or divergent paths, imaginative and innovative new thought can be experienced. Creative inquiry is a joyous tool to engage with our students collaboratively, and in consideration of the particular contexts and cultures of our unique learning communities.

Creative inquiries can also be used as a throughline, or a way to follow a central thought. A choreographer might use a throughline as a way to convey a narrative or story through movement. Educators can apply throughlines, or thoughtlines, to ensure lessons are interconnected over time. Using a creative inquiry as a throughline can encourage us, and our students, to bring our own artful curiosities alongside our expertise in content. Choreographer Twyla Tharp has called this the "spine" of the work and encourages artists to understand that all parts ought to connect back to this central concept (2009). Our lessons and units also can be unified with creative inquiry as a spine, for example: "How do scientists understand the world around them?" Or "How can history bridge us to our future?" Our throughline and creative inquiry for this book is "Do my lessons love my students?"

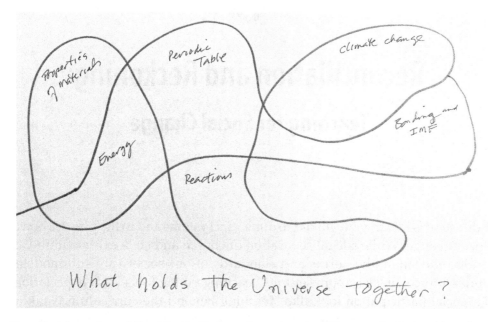

Figure 5.2 Science throughline. What holds the universe together? Photograph of science-based creative inquiry.

Bibliography

Tharp, T. (2009). *The Creative Habit: Learn It and Use It For Life*. Simon & Schuster.

6

Reconciliation and Reckoning

Teaching for Social Change

Education is inextricably linked to our social systems and to the progression of social change. While a legal separation of church and state exists within U.S. public education, the norms and standards of our society are still modeled and reinforced in classroom settings, teaching young folks what expectations for social participation look like. Teaching beyond the curriculum is taking place in every moment, sometimes consciously but mostly unconsciously.

Reckoning and reconciliation are actions that go hand in hand, and it's hard to get to one without the other. A focus on reconciliation without reckoning with the underlying harms that led to imbalances of power, for example, will struggle to be truly restorative. Reckoning without love can lead to a recreation of oppression and harm. The practice of social analysis (the ability to read the dynamics and power structures found through race, status, rank, class, age, etc.) while valuing and honoring intersectional cultural experiences is an example of how we can reckon and reconcile.

Reckoning

It makes sense as educators that we are able to conduct a thorough examination of the underlying unconscious messages implicit in our teaching, the "systems and structures in place so long, they look like the natural order

DOI: 10.4324/9781003301226-8

of things" that Isabel Wilkerson speaks of in her book *Caste: The Origins of Our Discontents* (2020). Systems and procedures in our classrooms may seem morally neutral, but when we examine them closely, we find that particular behavioral policies are linked to erroneous beliefs that apply carceral practices or dog training principles to our children. It's the same with the content we teach. If we don't reckon with scripted content that reproduces dehumanizing stereotypes, such as a harmful math worksheet in which students count the number of "Indians" for "Thanksgiving," it will be a long walk toward reconciliation.

When approaching reconciliation, teachers need to lead with their strengths. It is our strengths that will help us to move through confronting the uncomfortable truths of our unjust past, especially within a U.S. educational context. Reconciliation means we face the legacies of genocide, enslavement, and caste reinforced by unequal education from the very start. Thomas Jefferson suggested an elementary public education system for males of European descent only. Native American children were taken from their families to boarding schools in order to "civilize" them and were disallowed participation in Indigenous ceremonies and traditional practices, which were made illegal up until 1978 (Dunbar-Ortiz, 2015). How can we possibly reconcile this kind of past with a brighter future?

Land Acknowledgement

Land acknowledgement is an important first step in reckoning with our collective past. It's a way to shift power by publicly remembering historical truths and trauma. Land acknowledgement also acknowledges that Indigenous people are still present on unceded territories across the Americas, and for centuries have maintained interconnected stewardship principles with the land. We have long advocated for a regular and consistent practice of Indigenous and Native land acknowledgement in formal social contexts and gatherings and also for moving from acknowledgement into restorative actions.

UN Decree

The United Nations Declaration on the Rights of Indigenous Peoples was adopted in 2007, with 144 nation states in favor, 11 abstaining, and 4 votes against. The four countries who voted against adoption, Australia, Canada, New Zealand, and the United States, are all considered settler colonialist nations. These four later reversed their stance. The declaration establishes human rights and liberties for the present and future survival, dignity and well-being of the Indigenous peoples of the world (United Nations, 2008).

An opening acknowledgement of the Indigenous land we stand on includes acknowledgement of the particular Indigenous local community and tribal affiliations, particularly in North America and other settler colonialist contexts. It may also include an acknowledgement of systemic violence, enslavement, and historic profit from the unpaid labor of Indigenous, Black, and Brown bodied people.

Many school communities and organizations we have worked with have expanded the act of making this statement into a greater living relationship with social justice actions and engaging more deeply with the land itself within the curriculum. In doing so, we have seen an increased number of educational communities connecting directly with local Indigenous tribes and affiliations through efforts to incorporate cultural arts practices with guidance from experts, and even to participate in rematriation or "land back" efforts.

The context for a liberatory education can be set by incorporating the regular practice of Indigenous and Native land acknowledgement. Consider engaging with this practice by opening your learning environment with a ritual that acknowledges the land you stand on in a developmentally appropriate way with your students. Have them join you in research about and connection with the tribes present in your region and recreate your own statement based on your research. Notice how over time your actions may evolve to embody this acknowledgement as a living practice, within and beyond the classroom. Look into the historical contexts and current practices around acknowledging land, and also consider how to eventually move this practice into restorative action. Use the UN Declaration of Indigenous Rights as a core text for artistic research. We have seen many teachers practice land acknowledgement alongside or in place of the pledge of allegiance. See where it leads your students' interests and inquiries, and consider following thoughts and ideas that arise in meaningful ways.

Reconciliation Through the Bridge That Is *Conocimiento*

Epistemology, or how we orient ourselves through knowledge, understanding, ethics and beliefs, is a way of describing our construction of reality. It's our personal grasp of the way things are, and it has been nurtured in large part through our languages and cultures of origin. A culturally responsive education understands and incorporates epistemological frames from our students' cultural lineages. Our current classroom practices already sit in a cultural context within a construction of reality that is not universal. Our classrooms are also situated within regional and neighborhood cultures with distinct understandings of what school is for and how it works. This is all before we get to the caregiver and student level of language and culture. Developing cultural empathy around customs, relational and behavior norms, and orientation to knowledge, ethics and the cosmos is a far more responsive and loving curricular practice than bringing in representation through the 5 Fs: food, fashion, festivals, famous people, and flags (Hall, 1976).

Conocimiento in translation means knowledge or conscience in Spanish. Social scientist Gloria Anzaldúa explains the path of *conocimiento* as an epistemology, by which she meant an inquiry and understanding into the nature of existence that bridges cultural experiences and can be reached through creative acts (Anzaldúa, 2015). *Conocimiento* is Anzaldúa's term for the use of the body, mind, and spirit to expand knowledge and wisdom through a bridging process of internal and external reckoning. *Conocimiento*, as she describes it, calls on intellectual pursuit as only one aspect of our emotional, social, cultural, physical, artistic, ancestral, and cosmological understandings. *Conocimiento* is the practice of building our consciousness, the art of knowing through all aspects of being a human. Anzaldúa affirms that we learn through our senses, our environments, our emotions, and our many intersectional cultural identities, and that together, through acts of creation, we increase our ability to make meaning by sharing our wisdom in collective practice.

Much like the practice of land acknowledgement, *conocimiento* serves as both reckoning and reconciliation. It advances our understanding of self, other, and community within shared and discrete cultural contexts. *Conocimiento* as an educational practice sets the tone for learning, activates familiarity between individuals, and creates a sense of larger community.

Conocimiento in an educational context is the place where we ask individuals to enter into a caring learning space, release barriers that prevent connection with others, and invoke memory, story, and strengths from each individual in order to build meaningful, authentic relationships across the community. This point of connection is an invaluable place to return when the path of learning hits up against internal or external points of friction. It can provide a group or individual with courage, wisdom, and a reminder of our shared intersectional humanity.

It is our positionality (as a gendered person, as a person with a disability, as a person of color, as a person of a dominant caste, as a person of wealth, etc.) that informs how we experience the world at large. It is the starting point for referencing the world and the point from which we can choose to evolve beyond the limitation of social constructions. This has been help-fully referred to by psychologist and theater practitioner Letitia Nieto as our social "rank," which she distinguishes from our surface level status and our inner core of authentic power (Nieto, 2010).

Linked to intersectionality, positionality is an individual's location in rela-tion to others within a social system. The identification and naming of posi-tionality or rank can be a powerful tool in bringing awareness to the privilege afforded to differing groups and to processes of othering and belonging in particular. Examination and analysis of one's location within a system of inequity can lead to the disruption of implicit bias.

The socioemotional learning movement is a frame that points us in the direction of integration of multiple ways of knowing (Srinivasan, 2021). If you are familiar with this approach in education, you will likely have a fond-ness for the undertaking of *conocimiento* in an educational context. It is a way we can construct human centered learning that encompasses building knowl-edge beyond our prioritization of brain-bound thinking.

Creative Inquiries
> *How might I focus on the work of reckoning, racial healing and social change through shared knowledge, power analysis, and exploration of narrative and lineage?*
>
> *In what ways does my teaching practice address and disrupt social inequities while attending to the critical need for reflection and healing?*

Bibliography

Anzaldúa, G. E. (2015). *Light in the Dark/Luz en lo Oscuro: Rewriting Identity, Spirituality, Reality*. (A. Keating, Ed.). Duke University Press.

Dunbar-Ortiz, R. (2015). *An Indigenous Peoples' History of the United States*. Beacon Press.

Hall, E. T. (1976). *Beyond Culture*. Anchor Books.

Nieto, L. (2010). *Beyond Inclusion, Beyond Empowerment: A Developmental Strategy to Liberate Everyone*. Cuetzpalin.

Srinivasan, M. (2021). *Integrating SEL Into Every Classroom: The What, Why, and How*. WW Norton.

United Nations. (2008). *The United Nations Declaration on the Rights of Indigenous Peoples*. https://www.un.org/esa/socdev/unpfii/documents/DRIPS_en.pdf

Wilkerson, I. (2020). *Caste: The Origins of Our Discontents*. Random House.

7

Artistic Research

Essential Methodologies for Knowledge Acquisition

When the arts are decentralized and perceived as non-essential, certain groups of students are excluded from participating, often increasing their marginalization within the school ecosystem and disconnecting them from their own vitality and voice.

— Julie Kendig, RISE Research & Evaluation

Artists often follow a creative inquiry or set of questions that guide their art making, even if those questions are based in explorations of the medium. While creative inquiry often applies itself to considering the whole, artistic research is the process one might take to get to a satisfactory answer. Artistic research involves acquiring the knowledge sets necessary to create works of art. Artistic research also, however, applies the methods, techniques, and practices found in the arts to any learning process.

DOI: 10.4324/9781003301226-9

Figure 7.1 Drawing as research.

Artists change our world. In practice, they are often deep observers and connection makers. They find creative solutions. They open up pathways for others to make meaning of the world around them. They drive hope, they insist on change, they insist on thinking and feeling, all which support and develop us as people.

Artists can vacillate between disciplines. They often notice particular things around them, develop curiosities about these noticings, and then use a particular medium or form to make meaning of the curiosity, creating works that might arrive at either more questions or point to some answers. When multimedia artists activate observation, they often make and create through the discipline that will provide them the most insight. For example, artist Mark Dion takes on the behaviors of a biologist in order to create his living ecosystem art pieces. His research methods include knowing as much about biology as a working biologist.

Einstein employed artistic research to problem solve equations and theories. He specifically used a form of embodied imagination to figure out key missing ideas. To figure out the theory of relativity, he at one point imagined riding on a sunbeam from the sun to the planet. He moved his body the way he thought the electrons would move, and observed what natural inclinations happened, meaning he let the information come through this body. We have embodied imagination to thank for inspiring aspects of Einstein's theory of relativity.

The Power of Artistic Research

After starting and running the theater arts program and student theater company OakTechRep for a decade at the large, comprehensive public school Oakland Technical High School (where famous alumni included Huey Newton), Jessa's colleague, choreographer, and friend Ena Dallas stepped into the role, expanding the work in devised and verbatim theater they had practiced in the company since 2005. In 2019, Ena and the student company focused their artistic research on a rich history associated with the school itself.

The Apollos were students from the class of 1981 at Oakland Technical High School, who were responsible for getting Martin Luther King Jr's birthday made into a state holiday. It started when one of the students asked, "Why aren't there any holidays for Black people?" and followed that inquiry all the way. Their efforts during their high school years eventually led to it becoming the national holiday that we have now. Our artistic research process began in 2019 with our student theater company conducting a series of interviews with the Apollos, their teacher Tay MacArthur, and various folks who supported them. These interviews became the foundation of our full-length play and were used to create dialogue, inform character development, make musical choices, inspire movement, and shape an interpretive, cohesive narrative.

Through this creative process, students made personal connections to the Apollos' stories. Many actors had the epiphany that they too could do something great at their age and wanted to inspire other students to share in this feeling of what's possible. Their intention became to empower others through honoring the Apollos' story.

It was meaningful to witness, through the process of co-creating this play, the respect that grew between my students and the elders they interviewed. The more time they spent with each other, the more they revered one another, and a mutual cross-generational respect blossomed.

The performances took place on the weekend before the MLK Jr. birthday holiday in 2020. On opening night, city officials and school board members came and honored the Apollos. There was pride that current students wanted to uplift the Apollos' story.

One student actor, poet Samuel Getachew, played an Apollo who he had interviewed several times. Samuel combined the interviewee's words with his own interpretations to create a poetic monologue. I wasn't sure how the interpretation would land; however, one moment that was most meaningful to me was watching this man, the Apollo, run up to Samuel after the show with tears streaming down his face and bringing Samuel into a big bear hug, saying "That's right, that's right. ..."

This form of artistic research can provide an opportunity for human beings to authentically see one another, to witness each other. This can lead to more compassion, connection, and the profound ability to better understand the human experience. The theater artists in this process worked with the sole intention of understanding what it was the other person was trying to convey. There is power in this type of connection through artistic process in an educational setting.

– Ena Dallas, Arts Educator/Administrator

This is a powerful example of artistic research shared by two generations of learners. The first generation explored a question of great social significance, which led them to take action. The second generation engaged in artistic research through the interview process, then processed the information and knowledge from the interviews, then used creative expression and interpretation to develop a script, and finally shared a performance piece which showcased their understanding.

I had absolutely no idea what artistic research meant when I was learning about the role of arts in education. In fact, I had no idea that the arts required research! In my worldview at that time, the arts were skills and passions that you choose to experience because it provided something in you, a feeling of love, joy, expansion, etc. It wasn't in my consciousness that the arts require sophisticated levels of thinking and processing. In order to create, you acquire knowledge and know how, you experiment, risk, explore. You persist and stay consistent, you seek out that which you do not yet understand.

– Mariah

Knowledge is often shared through experiences specific to our cultural contexts, passed from one generation to another, and grows through the innovation each new generation brings into the practice. Artistic research is an ancient and modern form of technological innovation, where culture is built and expanded alongside our knowledge and skill sets.

How does any of this translate to the rallying cry of providing a "twenty-first century education" to the next generation? Zaretta Hammond's important and influential work on culture and the science of learning in education has some clues. In *Culturally Responsive Teaching and the Brain*, Hammond reminds us that human brains require active neurons in order to learn anything new.

Learning is often a social activity, and some research has found that the brain produces hormones helpful to memory and knowledge acquisition through engaging in relational creative processes (mirroring, pattern making, games) with others. (Hammond, 2014) Those who have had the experience of being nurtured by a master teacher or mentor know that in order to learn, it can be helpful to feel as though someone cares enough to teach us.

> Techniques in tap dance require a lot of study. As a child I pushed myself to develop the abilities needed to make riffs, slams, cramp rolls, draw backs, shuffles and flaps in order to perfectly showcase my talents. By the time I was fourteen, I knew I had the skills needed to create a dance with my best friend in class. We spent our afternoons making up choreography for the end of the year recital. We even designed our costumes: a bow tie and white shirts tied in a side knot over our black leotards. It was a source of pride for us to develop our own tap dance routine and have our names printed in the program as dancers and choreographers.
>
> – Mariah

> As a young actor, I apprenticed for a short time with Maestro Antonio Fava, who hailed from a lineage of performers doing masked socio-political street theater (commedia dell'arte). This work was primarily focused on rehearsing physical skill sets to replicate gestures and forms in the physical body, learning about the traditional characters and scenarios that make up the form. We were also trained in the disciplines of acrobatics, tango, and other performing arts skills that would allow us to have an artful capacity with which to simply improvise our entire performances later. In this case, divergent and convergent thinking were applied within the context of relationship and lineage, which is how cultural arts have traditionally been handed down. His own small children would often attend class with us, and even offer critique! As the daughter of a sculptor, my own childhood memories include an immersion in clay dust and studio time, and my own two daughters likewise have been raised on theater rehearsal hall floors. In this way, the contemporary arts have been my culture, and have served as a cultural experience my students and I could share in, and continue to shape together.
>
> – Jessa

Our students may not learn traditional drumming rhythms or ceremonial regalia design from us (or they may!), but they might engage in building out a digital media film with one another that draws them into the content knowledge, helps them to make decisions and problem solve, creates an opportunity for collective learning, and potentially influences culture shifts within their sphere and offers something new to the world. Veteran teacher Andy West recalls seeing academic outcomes from middle school students he had not seen in his 28 years of teaching once he applied artistic research to his statistics lessons, where students created 'zines based on exponential rates of increase in a fictional zombie apocalypse. Artistic research, as it applies to learning, is connected to authentic meaning making and contains memorable applications.

> I remember getting to explore topics and themes that had to do with education and equity; through movement, visual art, image. To see the ways that they (Studio Pathways) are centering issues of equity, racial justice, access, and decolonial practice with the integrative arts is like permission given.
> – Jahan Khalighi, Director of Programs at Chapter 510

Beyond Standard

Although it is an aspiration and intention that educators not be limited by a strict adherence to the concept of standards, the U.S. national arts standards frameworks are, much like the Studio Habits of Mind, at their most distilled form, processes and actions that promote thinking: Create, Produce/Perform/Present, Respond, and Connect. The understanding that even national standards are rooted not in discrete knowledge sets and concrete goals, but in actions and practice, is a reframe in the minds of many classroom teachers. These guideposts ask us to observe, analyze, conceptualize, conceive, organize, synthesize, refine, make meaning, and relate. These are all actions taken within the artistic research process.

Unfortunately, educational standards are linked to rigid structural systemic regulations and have often been weaponized or accompany a feeling of mystery or inadequacy for many teachers. For some, standards have become a measuring stick used to alienate, instead of serving as guides on the side that support our teaching and learning practice. Even the term "standard" is something that lacks the intention and aspiration of a liberatory educational frame. By incorporating artistic research processes into our classroom practices, we generally are able to meet and even exceed standards set by outside authorities not familiar with our contexts and student cultures.

Creative Inquiries
> *Where can I employ artistic research as a relational creative practice I offer my learners?*
> *How can methodologies found in the cultural and contemporary arts be used to explore content area concepts and increase my students' cognitive capacities?*

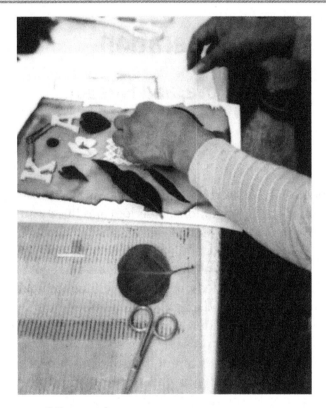

Figure 7.2 Cyanotype as artistic research.

Bibliography

Hammond, Z. (November 13 2014). *Culturally Responsive Teaching and the Brain: Promoting Authentic Engagement and Rigor Among Culturally and Linguistically Diverse Students.* Corwin Press.

Nationalartsstandards.org. (2023). Home. https://www.nationalartsstandards.org/

Dion, M. (n.d.). Art21. https://art21.org/artist/mark-dion/

8

Liberation

Art, Love, and Freedom

Just as our liberation is intertwined with one another's, so education and liberation are interlaced companions. Freedom and liberty are core narratives held with many disparate meanings in the social imagination of the United States. The concept of freedom, and our experiences with or without it, have led us to varied notions of what liberation means and what its embodiment looks like. What if we expanded our notions and conceptual understanding of liberation in mind, body, and spirit?

Take a moment and consider what freedom means to you. When have you felt most free? What qualities were present? We recognize that a sense of freedom or liberation feels different to each of us depending on our lived circumstances and positionality in society. How might it then be a universal orientation in our lesson design? Our answer, yet again, is through love and art.

Asking ourselves if our lessons love our students is also asking whether our lessons increase or decrease liberation in the short and long term. What if the practice of freedom was a daily practice in the classroom? As educators who have taught with a belief system grounded in social justice, our own meaning of liberatory education is activated through the building of a critical and creative mind.

Liberatory pedagogy is not a set of instructions but rather an embodied stance or orientation woven throughout our teaching methods. Liberation requires the ability to trust in our students enough to create a container they eventually can and should outgrow. By intentionally applying creativity to

DOI: 10.4324/9781003301226-10

the lessons we create, our lessons will not only remove obstacles to joy for our students but for ourselves. If there is no joy in the teaching, there will be no joy in the learning. Liberatory lessons will not only love our students but love us too.

It can be humbling to attempt to practice education as liberatory when we ourselves do not feel free. Liberatory educator bell hooks in *Teaching to Transgress* named that self-actualization was a necessary condition for teaching in a liberatory way. By modeling and enacting our own sense of liberation in our own lives, perhaps through creative practice or artful pursuit of our intellectual passions, our students can come to know what freedom looks like for themselves.

Self-actualization can be experienced through creativity, in developing our own acts of artistry large and small, but also in witnessing and taking in the artistry of others. Witnessing the creative acts of others can in and of itself be liberating, as we see our humanity affirmed or our souls and spirits illuminated by the liberation of another.

The entire canon of African American artistry in particular can be seen exemplary of great acts of liberation, where often art, love, and liberation look very similar. In artistic lineage, the goal is not always art for art's sake; it has often been art for liberation's sake, such as in the passing down of cultural knowledge through song, or through dance forms that allow historically constrained bodies to feel and to be free.

This is not to mistake educational liberation for absolute, unlimited anarchy. There is great power in limits. When we invite students to improvise in a jazz quartet, it is important that we have given them enough prior knowledge and instrumental technique and rhythmic structure to set them free. When we set up an open mic on campus each Friday for spoken word poetry and rap battles at lunch, it is important that we have prepared and entrusted our students with the responsibility of playing for a school audience within a set of boundaries and limits and given circumstances. We can trust our students to try on a freedom that looks like increased community responsibility. We can invite them to enact their newfound freedom for their peers, their families, and their teachers, knowing it can in turn increase a sense of freedom for others.

Community murals co-designed and painted by students can feel liberatory, giving space for young artists to make their own public marks in service of their voice and self-expression. Public performances can also increase a sense of freedom of self-expression. Theater games can also feel liberatory, especially when silliness and play are invoked where students might otherwise feel hypervigilant about showing up with pressure to "be grown" or "look cool." When working on oral presentations, sometimes volume or a sense of vocal confidence can feel challenging for many students. There can be great liberation in the invitation to "try and disturb the classroom next door with how loudly you read your poem."

When we grow a mind that thinks artistically, we grow our capacity to be free. We can widen our access to and understanding of knowledge, exploring internal and external worlds that mesh to provide us a more vast experience. The very nature of expanding our awareness involves critical thinking and creative questioning of assumptions about the world in which we live. We acquire knowledge through curiosity, research and making, and insight through reflection and community. Viewing the world through the perspective of an artist, we can expand our idea of what is possible, and experience greater range in the act of being human. Artist Alok V. Menon tells their audiences that authenticity is an orientation, not a destination (Menon, 2021). We say the same about the role of building a liberatory stance as an educator: Liberation is an orientation, not a destination.

Mia Birdsong invited a group of friends and community members to learn more about her next inquiry about freedom: "I came across these two facts about freedom that I have not been able to stop thinking about for the last four years. The first fact is that the word "freedom" and the word "friendship" have the same etymological root. It's a Sanskrit root, which means beloved. And that in and of itself, I was just like, what? Like freedom and friendship are connected, are rooted together. The second fact is that pre-1500s—in pre-U.S. Western context—an enslaved person was understood as not free, not just because they were in bondage, but because they were separated from their people. To be free was understood as being in a connected community. Freedom was something you experienced with other people. And these facts both blew my mind and totally resonated with me." As I sat listening to my friend's wisdom, I thought about all the ways that relationship is key to any effort in liberatory education. This kind of freedom focuses on what we can create together, instead of what we can achieve alone. Therefore, our classroom spaces become a place to practice and create freedom in community.

– Mariah

Paulo Friere's idea of a liberatory pedagogy involved practicing freedom from fear. Educators are often good rule followers, or good test takers, and practicing liberation can feel chaotic or even dangerous or out of control. Freedom might sometimes be the opposite of following the rules and drawing inside the lines. Personal comfort might be stretched when class volume levels increase, or conversely when group calm and quiet thinking time is trusted, or even when movement is invited into the space through both structure and flow.

How do we impose our will less in order to teach freedom? We can teach students, and ourselves, to trust conscious awareness more and external systems less. Cultivate experiences of autonomy by nurturing creative and critical thought which lead to a sense of community responsibility. Honor lineages when appropriate, but not with a false respect based on compliance or fear of authority, which we often consciously or unconsciously pass along to our students.

Art as an Antidote

Artists have power. Historical patterns have shown us that when a country leans into authoritarianism, the artists are the first to be persecuted. The artist Ai Wei Wei lived under surveillance of his government who eventually burned down his studio, jailed him, and then put him under house arrest. He now lives in a political asylum and is considered one of the world's most powerful artists in his dissent to authoritarianism.

Teachers may not have the power to *reform* education in general, but we do have the power to teach from an artful stance that values liberation. Teachers, when first practicing with the liberatory role of arts in education, often seek permission to make attempts and explore how to do it well. We have the power to give ourselves permission to teach from this perspective, particularly in defiance of classrooms and schooling that repeat oppressive forms of practice.

SPIRAL Creative Inquiries for Review
  Studio Pathway: How will a studio setting be designed in my classroom?
  Creative Inquiry: What are the core inquiries within my content that relate to shared culture, and how can my students and I explore them creatively?
  Reconciliation: What is the history and lineage of the content being studied or information being introduced? Whose stories and knowledge sets are uplifted and centered in the curriculum? Is societal power considered?
  Artistic Research: How will students artfully take action and make meaningful explorations toward understanding the creative inquiries more fully?
  Love and Liberation: What joyous, artful demonstrations of knowledge and learning can take place, both throughout and at the culmination of study? What will be created and produced? How will students respond and connect?

Bibliography

Birdsong, M. (2022). Freedom's Revival, Virtual Presentation.
Friere, P. (1970). *Pedagogy of the Oppressed*. Continuum Publishing Corporation.
hooks, b. (2014). *Teaching To Transgress*. Routledge. https://doi.org/10.4324/9780203700280
Kozak, N. (n.d.). *Ai Weiwei —*. Art21. https://art21.org/artist/ai-weiwei/
Menon, A. V. (2021). 2021 New Years Resolutions. https://www.pixstory.com/story/alok-vaid-menon-2021-new-years-resolutions/24390

Part Three

The Core Four

Part Three:

The Core Four

Figure P3.1 Title page, Section Three.

9

The Core Four

Foundational Concepts

The *Core Four* are four foundational themes that serve as the underpinnings of our SPIRAL Framework: Power, Narrative, Lineage, and Embodiment. The Core Four can be flexibly invoked to interrogate power dynamics, employ narrative strategies to shift power, and understand relational, intellectual, artistic, and cultural lineages through the strengths we find there. The Core Four help us to interrogate where things come from, including which lineages contain power, which narratives can be embodied for a brighter future, and which lineages, dominant narratives, and harmful power structures need to be let go of. The Core Four are where we can look to see evidence of transformation in interpersonal and cultural shifts. The Core Four have continued to evolve and serve as foundational principles and measures for culturally responsive outcomes in our work.

Applying the Core Four

Partner arts organization Chapter 510 & The Dept. of Make Believe has used Studio Pathways' Core Four as a main throughline in their program delivery. They have focused one consecutive year of study on each theme, creating whole books of poems related to each, uplifting the works of the young BIPOC and LGTBQIA+ students they serve.

DOI: 10.4324/9781003301226-12

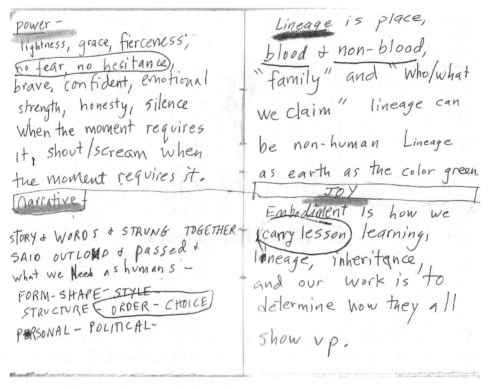

power –
lightness, grace, fierceness;
no fear, no hesitance,
brave, confident, emotional
strength, honesty, silence
when the moment requires
it, shout/scream when
the moment requires it.

Narrative :

STORY & WORDS & STRUNG TOGETHER
SAID OUTLOUD & passed &
what we need as humans –
FORM – SHAPE – STYLE
STRUCTURE – ORDER – CHOICE
PERSONAL – POLITICAL –

Lineage is place,
blood & non-blood,
"family" and "who/what
we claim" lineage can
be non-human. Lineage
as earth as the color green.

JOY

Embodiment is how we
carry lesson learning,
lineage, inheritance,
and our work is to
determine how they all
show up.

Figure 9.1 Student study of the Core Four from Chapter 510.

Many school sites, such as the Wildcat Canyon Community School in El Sobrante, California, have used the Core Four frame flexibly as an assessment tool to self-evaluate classroom practices or to conduct "equity walkthroughs" looking for how power, lineage, narrative, and embodiment are represented in space and classroom design.

Creative Inquiry
How do you currently experience power, narrative, lineage, and embodiment
playing out in your own teaching and learning environment?

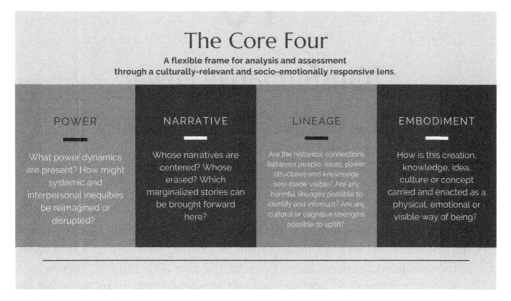

Figure 9.2 Graphic of the Core Four.

Bibliography

Chapter 510. (n.d.). Chapter 510 | A made-in-Oakland youth writing, book-making & publishing center. https://www.chapter510.org/

Wildcat Canyon Community School. (2018, July 9). Wildcat Canyon Community School | Educating the Whole Child; Wildcat Canyon Community Waldorf School. https://wildcatcanyon.org/

10

Transformative Power
Addressing Social Power Dynamics

Most humans have experienced "othering" based on external identity markers that meant they were excluded from belonging in a felt and real sense. Even those whose markers have them at the top of a ranked, hierarchical caste system within their societal context in some areas may have felt the slight of being last in others, last picked for a team at recess due to a disability, or internally battling a history of adverse childhood experiences or trauma that cannot be read on the skin. These kinds of lived experiences, if processed through our capacity to empathize, instruct us to help transform power.

Transformative power involves deciphering a complex series of interwoven internal and external conditions. Transformative power supports our change from one state of being to another. When we integrate new knowledge, acquire sound judgment, and activate new behaviors or ideas, we strengthen our capacity for the embodiment of transformative power. This is the type of power we ultimately want to lead and teach through. This form of power doesn't hinge on needs of the ego but concerns itself with growth of our experience as humans. This is a loving stance to orient ourselves from.

Education in the United States was originally designed to amass power for an elite class of white bodied men to advance their thinking and ensure their power over a racialized caste system. Until 1834, anti-literacy laws made it illegal to teach a Black person to read (Wilkerson, 2020). It is often taught that these early social designers were just "of their time" and did not know any better than to consider the rights of all human beings. It is harder to

DOI: 10.4324/9781003301226-13

understand that these choices were deliberate and executed by implementing destructive power over others and Earth.

> On a quiet evening in 2008, I sat with the poet Tongo Eisen-Martin. I was sharing my first essay on inequity in education when he stopped and said, "What you're failing to mention is that we are sitting in a white supremacist design." I took a deep breath. These were words I wasn't used to saying out loud or including in my arguments about race and equity in education. They were jarring words, and I lived my grayscale life avoiding them as much as possible. I pressed Tongo to explain, because the truth was, I had not allowed myself to conceptualize our society as driven by white supremacy. Tongo carried on conveying the founding fathers as leaders that deliberately choose power and profit through the domination of land and resources. He described the white elites as barbarians who approved and commanded the enslavement of 12.6 million Africans and the genocide of Indigenous peoples. Hearing the narrative of our nation told in this way revealed a clarity I had been afraid to face. It meant that I had huge steps to take in my knowledge of history, it meant admitting that there were still more uncovered perspectives I had failed to grasp, and it meant that I could not unsee it. We live in a historical framework designed by a narrow imagination. Our social framework was designed primarily by white-bodied elite men to serve and uphold an unequal operational system, imported from European contexts. It is through the practice of expanding our imaginations that we can remember the contributions that have been lost and stolen over time and further our ability to devise the future.
>
> – Mariah

Transformative power generates action or change and can be felt when we work in connection with each other. You've likely witnessed transformative power when you have students collaborate on a project or produce a shared assignment. If transformative power was thoughtfully distributed according to strengths within the group, students likely had a meaningful learning experience. The act of teaching itself is ideally an engagement with transformative power.

Power and Caste Consciousness

I was thrilled to attend the on-the-ground movement conference organized by Allied Media in 2014 held at Wayne State University in Michigan, where my grandmother went to college. I flew out with one of the instructors in the Integrated Learning Specialist program I was managing out of the Alameda County Office of Education at the time. We were sharing a room together, excited to have quality time to get to know one other. As we hopped around the conference day, we would connect back at the dorm room and excitedly report what we heard, what we saw, and make recommendations to each other.

During our second day there we had an experience she and I will never forget. We had both earmarked a workshop entitled "Making Home." The description of it sounded nurturing and wonderfully complex. The expansiveness of the university's campus meant long walks between workshops. There was also a strict limit on the amount of people allowed in a workshop, which meant that if you were late, you were not getting in. I knew I was going to be late for the "Making Home" workshop. I sped up my gait, stopping to ask for directions a few times for its location. As I neared the door to the workshop, I saw my colleague Beth clipping at a fast pace to reach the door from the opposite direction. We eyed each other and grinned. Then we saw the facilitator step out of the door frame, reach for the door knob and begin to close it, which meant she was at capacity. "Wait!" I yelled, "Can we come in?" I gestured to Beth, who was equidistant to the door in the opposite direction. Just like in the movies when time slows down, which is how our brains record moments like these, I saw the facilita- tor look at me, look at Beth, turn back to me and say "Sorry, we are full." Then she looked again at me, and said, "You know what, come on in." And she turned to Beth and said, "Sorry, I'm giving space to Black bodies today." Beth's body took a moment to comprehend and immediately responded with "Yes, yes, of course." And she walked away. I, feeling stunned, said thank you to the facilitator and found a seat inside. At that moment, I experienced flashes of my childhood life in school. Flashes where I sat at the back, raising my hand, but never was called on. Flashes where I felt insignificant on the spectrum of my peers or dismissed because my Black body and spirit was not favored. Flashes of Matthew, who was both my neighbor and my classmate, a white bodied boy who would get selected over and over again and was adored by our teachers. I began to cry. The facilitator had barely begun her intro as I wiped away tears, trying to hide the reaction my body was having to have been specifically "chosen." This one moment was so significant that I don't remember much of the workshop. My mind and spirit were still processing this profound gesture.

As a practicing social justice educator, one of the elements that I have always tried to support my fellow colleagues in is how to see and navigate social power dynamics connected to caste (class, rank, status, gender, ability) in real time. In speaking with Beth, she mentioned the impacts that it had on her as well. We both experienced the transformative use of power in this moment, growing by leaps and bounds through one gesture that illuminated how our bodies carried our personal racialized identity markers. It's a memory neither of us have forgotten but have been *remarkably* impacted by as we continue to build our understanding of how we might dismantle caste expectations and move forward.

– Mariah

I already had many years of trainings and readings thinking about my privilege and racial oppression, proving that an embodied experience pushes us deeper than knowledge, into understanding. When I was turned away from the workshop as a white body, I had a wave of complicated emotions I hadn't experienced before. Because of this experience my capacity for difficult and uncomfortable situations grew tremendously, to the point where I love them, because I know they will profoundly change me and allow me to stretch into a better human. I am so thankful for it.

– Beth

Transformative power can be acutely felt when power is shifted purposefully through intentional disruptions of an assumed caste order. Art can operate as a third space where we are able to analyze, deconstruct, and reimagine power with great complexity through an artistic medium. This special sauce allows for social and interpersonal healing without directly invoking personal or historic harm. While creative practice in the classroom space is ideally a healing action, the intent of culturally responsive teaching and learning is not to directly delve into individual and collective psychological trauma. This would be inappropriate for any educator without therapeutic credentials, and even less appropriate for an educator working with students across caste hierarchies such as racialized oppressions. The work we display here is our praxis for personal healing, reflection, and building of a pedagogical frame that when embodied by adults will serve the range of learners we have in our classrooms.

Most often, internally while teaching, I would work with the theater practice of status exercises. I was taught by my own theater mentor,

Linda Lowry, that status in the theater, and perhaps in life, is an internal and external social ranking that can be "given or taken away." In schooling, much of the messaging to students revolves around the taking away of status, in the form of discipline policies, behavior management and other punitive concepts focused on control and even coercion. As a liberatory practitioner, I often work mindfully with status, most basically through the choreography of my own body within an educational space.

The theater on a campus where I taught in for a decade was initially a huge, dark, damp neglected 900-seat cavern, slowly resurrected from serving as a flooded storage area for the district during my tenure. There were initially no supplies, a few ancient stage lights that sparked when turned on and off, broken seats, and a torn and dirty main curtain that I was told was once gold. It was, ironically, an ideal teaching space. Although I was in the mentoring role of teacher and director, meaning I inherently had a position of power in relation to my students, I would stand in what was basically an orchestra pit, four feet below the stage. My students stood on the stage, four whole feet above me for many of the lessons, or otherwise standing in a circle alongside me in empty space, where they lead their own vocal and physical warm up rituals, once established at the top of the year. This space very literally gave them a higher status than me, placing them upstage and center, if not yet in a functioning limelight.

When we were not working in the theater, I could replicate this experience by taking a kneeling or seated position in the classroom, where I had removed all of the desks. Our opening ritual in the classroom was a physical and vocal warmup (with consideration of varying needs and abilities) in a circle, journal writing on floor pillows in areas of the room that felt comfortable to each student, and then varied audience/performer configurations appropriate for rehearsal and performance time.

Without knowing it at the time, I had taken what john a powell has termed a *Targeted Universalist* approach to the way I attempted to internally navigate power and status, meaning I consistently sought to decenter myself and students with relative power in caste hierarchy, and recenter those at the societal margins. Externally, I reframed power structures in the curriculum by intentionally selecting plays where Black-bodied female identified students, LGTBQIA+ actors and students on the autism spectrum could shine in leading roles, conducting what I would now call not color-blind, but caste-conscious casting.

– Jessa

If we don't see color or caste, we can't see oppressions, and we can't adjust power dynamics in our classrooms accordingly. Building an awareness of and attunement to the implications of the caste system, while proceeding to teach our students as if the rules that govern that system do not apply, is a lifelong art. Providing subtle and overt course corrections to recenter non-dominant learners within the classroom culture is key. This is what is meant by an applied targeted universalist approach. This is the liberty of which we speak.

Transformative Power for Lessons That Love Our Students

How do we define and implement transformative power in our teaching? Transformation requires the work of breaking patterns, understanding history and culture, understanding intersectionality, having clarity around how our lineages play out over time, and the intentional formation of explicit belonging and beloved community.

Power

Figure 10.1 Heart and power image.

Our own study of "belonging" took hold while developing curricular work with john a. powell's Othering and Belonging Institute at UC Berkeley. The work of this institute investigates policies, practices, and approaches for how we can move away from power structures that create othering and toward power structures that build belonging. With intentional vision for an outcome of cultures of care, we can backwards design pedagogical practices and methods that are situated in a frame of transformative power.

Addressing Social Power Dynamics

Racialized and gender-based power dynamics are two very common, specific social power dynamics that show up in most of our learning spaces. There are similar power dynamics that show up in most of the facilitated spaces we lead, and likely show up for you in many gatherings. Have you ever noticed during a meeting, a conference setting, or workshop experience that as soon as a facilitator turns over the space for the audience to respond, the first person to speak will typically be the person with the most perceived status or rank in the room? This is a researched phenomenon. If someone with low perceived status or rank speaks up, it has been shown that they are seen as speaking "too much." We can analyze, intervene, and redirect imbalances of social power when it shows up.

We once had a team who didn't believe us until they did their own research. They reported back to us with embarrassment that they had noticed white-bodied men speaking first and promptly every time there was a staff meeting or learning session. This tends to be unconscious, as we have been raised in a context that gives power, rank, and status to those at the top of the caste hierarchy (Nieto, 2010). This is also not to say that power, rank, and status aren't useful and interchangeable. We can and do *remix* these concepts naturally through our everyday interactions.

Flip the Script

We first experienced the process we now refer to as "Flip the Script" with our colleague, who as a white, male, cisgender identified person working for social justice had done a lot of personal work to embody practices of trans-formative power. He walked us through the activation of how to address racialized and gender-based power dynamics in real time. For us it was a pleasure to put a name to what we had both already intuitively practiced, and it became a helpful tool for explicit instruction on how to teach it. Flip the

Script supports a reframe of how we show up for and with each other across intersectional identities in social contexts.

Flip the Script supports a transformative shift in power from the people who have been granted the most unearned power in our society to those with the least access. Flip the Script is often difficult to explain in settings where the system of caste-based inequity is not understood by all in the room, particularly people in positions of privilege who are used to holding the most space in conversation and/or decision making, or are new to understanding (especially) white and light-skinned or male privilege and the role it plays in perpetuating the silencing of marginalized people, particularly people of color and female-bodied folks around the world. To introduce Flip the Script, you might say something like:

> We are going to practice intentionally transforming power dynamics today. We will use the concept of Flip the Script as a way to reckon with our shared history of an unjust caste system that research has shown to confer status in group spaces by preferencing speakers who are perceived as male, taller, being more attractive, having job seniority, being a native English speaker and being white rather than anything else. To Flip the Script asks that anyone who has been granted the most unearned power in society based on intersecting factors of caste and rank (race, gender, age, religion, ability, citizenship, language, sexual orientation, class, etc.) will pause and listen to others speak before weighing in. We ask the group to internally assess their own internal and external identities and simply stay mindful throughout our time together. Who takes up the most and least airtime in group discussions and decisions? Flipping the Script asks that the floor be turned over to lead from the wisdom of those who have been most "othered" and who carry the burden of identity-based societal oppressions. We acknowledge that there can be discomfort around this ask regardless of your positionality or "situatedness," and invite this practice as a model for authentic reconciliation and as a path to create a culture of care and belonging.

Things to Consider

When people who have experienced multiple oppressions are asked to take up space, there is often a pause and hesitancy to do so. Something to consider is that people who come from collectivist cultures often hold space for the needs of the collective group by centering observation and listening as their primary role in group work. Another consideration is that members of nondominant groups are sometimes responding to internalized systems of oppression. Staying quiet and nonparticipation may be wise responses to uncertain power dynamics in space. It might be the first time in our lives that someone has considered centering our thoughts and feelings and knowledge first. It is a powerful practice to allow ample time for a response using the principles of Flip the Script, even if it feels uncomfortable to do so. Often folks who have the most unearned power may show discomfort and begin speaking if it stays quiet for too long. Restate the purpose and practice of using Flip the Script if this happens.

Practicing Flip the Script is not something that is appropriate for young learners. Meaning, we are not advocating that you necessarily explain the concept to your classroom of eight-year-olds. We do however advocate that you recognize how power is playing out between students based on their race, class, gender expression, ability, and intellectual abilities. Shifting power is more dependent on ways that you choreograph your classroom of students to have access to content, learning materials, and shared leadership of the classroom and in the development of social-emotional learning.

Lineage of Flip the Script

Many Indigenous peoples have deep rituals of respect around what we are calling Flip the Script. We acknowledge that this concept is not new and uplift it as but one practice to disrupt patterns of oppression. Generally, we have used this principle alongside *conocimiento* practice, and in the place of other social or cultural norm setting conversations.

Bibliography

Nieto, L. (2010). *Beyond Inclusion, Beyond Empowerment: A Developmental Strategy to Liberate Everyone*. Cuetzpalin.

Targeted Universalism. (n.d.). Berkeley.edu. https://belonging.berkeley.edu/targeted-universalism

Wilkerson, I. (2020). *Caste: The Origins of Our Discontents*. Random House.

11

Narrative

Examining Core Narratives in Education

In the arts, we often use narrative to help society imagine a new way forward. Stories are the primary way that we as humans make sense of the world. There are great stories many of us will never be privy to, having been passed down only through oral tradition. Stories cradle how we come to view and understand the living world around us and our positions in them. They hold and direct our thinking, actions, and responses.

Sometimes our stories are silent but visible to others, when they are accompanied by a scar or a limp in our gait—a visual cue that we have been through something and experience the world through a set of conditions or qualities. Sometimes they are invisible and yet core to our personal identity. These stories, these narratives that we are actively enmeshed with, hold complex ideas and understandings of who we are and where we are going.

Stories are a critical element in education. It's important that we understand the stories that we teach, not only in the literal sense of teaching reading and writing, but in the systemic sense in that we are teaching through narratives that we've been taught. We are teaching through our own story of the world. If our world has been narrowly focused, we must take on the task of not getting stuck in "the danger of a single story" as coined by Chimamanda Adichie in her famed TedTalk (Adichie, 2009). We remind ourselves, and our learners, that there is never a single story about anyone on the planet.

DOI: 10.4324/9781003301226-14

Expanding the Narrative/Narrative Intelligence

Narrative strategy and the wise application of narrative across sectors to shift culture, minds, hearts, and policies and practices is based on this: we humans learn best through story. Stories are the primary vehicle through which we intake and digest information. Narrative intelligence is finding, sharing, co-creating, and making meaning through narratives.

Long ago, and still in many places around the planet, a griot or storyteller might have shared a story around a fire, or traveled with rhyming songs to share wisdom and worldviews across communities. Currently, live performing arts continue to express the thoughts, feelings, ethics, experiences, and ideals of the griot. These experiences become encoded in our brains along with the meaning they convey. Even the "sage on the stage," while no longer considered a model for a holistic or equitable learning environment, still holds an important, limited place for inspiring learning within individuals who receive the messages of the speaker.

In current times, collective storytelling most often takes the form of mass media, usually specific to a particular genre within the medium of film or music or television. Each of these can be seen as a learning context or subject area shared by experts in the field, some more intentional than others. An excellent example of this type of teaching can be found in contemporary podcasts or TED talks. Here story and metaphor, or narratives, are often combined with compelling data, or knowledge sets from a particular lineage of thought and experience. The lessons, having been embodied and given voice to by the expert, are granted the power of a public platform.

In the 1960s and 1970s, many educators and artists who cared for children understood the burgeoning power of learning through mass media and pioneered children's television through programming such as *Sesame Street*, *Reading Rainbow*, *Mr. Rogers' Neighborhood*, *Electric Company*, and so on. This programming *intentionally* focused on creating literacy and cultures of care for children of diverse backgrounds through the visual and performing media arts—through arts such as story, song, puppetry, rhyme, patterns, and animation. Today we also see the use of media arts in online learning platforms; however, these spaces are often incomplete and lack a key element: the development of reciprocal relationship and care.

Stories drive change. There has been brilliant and influential work done by our partners at the Butterfly Lab/Race Forward and the Center for Cultural Power using narrative as a strategy to increase belonging, and it has been finally seen as a valuable, viable, and research-based approach to the work of transforming systems. The evolution of this principle of narrative, or storytelling, into realms that also ask us to take a good look at power, to reconcile often harmful lineages, and to actually embody our knowledge sets and ethics, or "walk our talk," is an important expansion of this principle.

Building Care Through Narratives

What are the stories you have about yourself? Perhaps yours is a complex story that vacillates between achievement, beauty, trauma, wholeness, and pain. Our inner life of stories become the lenses we experience our current realities through. What are the stories that highlight the bright moments of your life? What are the stories that you want to remain tucked away? How can your brightest moments carry you forward? How can the brightest moments of students' stories be given space? How can their stories be embedded in your curriculum?

Narratives in Our Teaching Practices

As a white-bodied, female identified theater educator who worked primarily with African-American students and in highly diverse spaces, I would rarely talk "at" my high school students directly about race, instead choosing plays and assignments that asked them to give thought and voice to their own intersectional experiences through pressing social and moral questions.

Our subject matter and material was sometimes representative of cultures or stories present in the lives my students had led, but once removed in some way, such as *Hamlet: Blood in the Brain*, a retelling by playwright Naomi Iizuka that set the Shakespearean story in Oakland, California during the 1980s. This was a time and place my students' caregivers had known well. It meant studying Shakespeare alongside studying Oakland in the 80s, listening to their music and asking family members and teachers about what hanging out at Lake Merritt was like "way back" then. This was a play that they ended up performing at CalShakes, Stanford, and internationally at the Edinburgh Festival Fringe to sold out houses. Narratives my students had grown up inside of made them temporary international theater stars.

Sometimes a play provided an adjacent imaginative fiction, a mask, or an exploration of the far away, the mythical, or the yet unknown. This could be through the writing of contemporary playwright Tarrell Alvin McCraney, whose characters in *In the Red and Brown Water* are contemporary archetypal representations of Yoruba gods and goddesses of the African diaspora, or the works of Richard Montoya in his scathing satire *American Night: The Ballad of Juan José*, about the racialized disparities immigrants face in pursuit of the American Dream. It meant bringing in professional artists representative of my student's cultural and ethnic identities to lead in an exploration of Iizuka's or McCraney's or Montoya's or Shakespeare's works, providing an embodied understanding of several forms of cultural and linguistic fluency.

– Jessa

What are the stories you have about your students? Teaching and learning is studied and practiced through many pedagogical beliefs. Some of these have been nurtured through philosophical understandings, science, and research. Some have been designed and practiced without doing the work of unearthing bias, historical impacts, and power dynamics between racialized cultures. When we focus our intellect and heart on the narratives that we teach, we can examine their culpability in reproducing harmful ideas and notions, negative impacts to the growth of learners, and how they might be shaping our collective culture at large. We can also seek out narratives that authentically represent healing and joy, representative of the values, ethics, and cultures of our students.

> *Creative Inquiries*
> *What narratives are visible in your classroom setting? In your school setting?*
> *What is the story, for example, behind the arrangement of desks in your classroom?*
> *What is the story of the school's daily schedule? What is the story of the physical environment?*

Narratives in the Content We Teach

There is a large transformative movement to diversify the books that we teach, alongside attempts by a few to stifle this progress. While representation remains important, it is critical to do the work of not only having diverse representation but to assess what type of representation is present. Reading stories where a Black character is present but never the main character, or is an enslaved character, or is exceptional to the extent that they are unrelatable, is telling a story through subtext. These stories can actually reinforce hierarchical caste structures. Pay attention and evaluate the narratives across the curricula for ways that larger social narratives are being reinforced. Who is getting prioritized? Who is left out? Who is pushed to the margins? Even stories that account for representation can often enforce dominant views. Pay attention to social power dynamics and how a story is being told.

Instead of teaching about the Founding Fathers in my first year of teaching, I decided to teach Global Citizens instead. I introduced Harriet Tubman, Martin Luther King Jr., Mahatma Gandhi, Jimmy Carter, Mother Teresa, Nelson Mandela, Jane Goodall. The newsletter to my classroom caregivers from 2006 reads: *Social Studies: Being a global citizen. This week we will study Cesar Chavez, Mahatma Gandhi, Harriet Tubman and Mother Teresa. Our focus will be showing citizenship through peaceful protest, honesty, helping others, and compassion. You can help your child with these concepts by modeling them at home or talking about people who model these qualities. You can also point out when your child is exhibiting these qualities so they know when they are being a responsible citizen. We have the wonderful privilege of having Lisa Serna (daughter of Joe Serna, former mayor of Sacramento) visiting our classroom on Tuesday April 4th. She will speak to the Kindergarten students about her father and his friendship with Cesar Chavez. Lisa will speak of her own memories of Cesar as he was a big part of her life. We look forward to her visit!*

Figure 11.1 Lisa Reinertson, *Cesar Chavez Memorial 2001*, Bronze 8.5 ft × 7 ft × 3 ft *Chavez Park, Sacramento City Hall, California.*

Looking back, I applaud my early efforts with this unit. As my teaching years went on, I expanded the notion of *citizenship* to be more responsive with a focus on local and global *community* members and their stories.

– Mariah

Narratives about Each Other

We hold many stories about each other and can easily slip into making assumptions and falling back into "single story" mode. To avoid this, we can explicitly develop a culture of belonging in which time is spent sharing stories and learning about who we are. What seems time consuming at first is returned exponentially when a class culture is vibrant and respectful, and disruptions and distractions are minimized down the road. In our work on explicit belonging and beloved community, we will walk you through the practice of verbatim theater to explore how you might engage in artistic research to build stronger cultures of connection.

Narratives about the Purpose of School

Exploring the existential purpose of an education is something that many teaching programs deem too political or personal or philosophical to address. If we don't examine what an education is for, then how can we be purposeful teachers in the first place? Continually examining narratives as an educator is core and sacred work. To be a teacher in this way is an extraordinary gift to the self and to the world.

> *Creative Inquiries*
> *What are the core narratives about schooling in the United States and what purpose do they serve?*
> *How do we disrupt dominant, one-sided narratives, and embody nuanced and complex narratives that serve and authentically represent students?*
> *How might we expand a collective imagination about the purpose of education and develop new narratives for our time?*

Bibliography

Adichie, C. N. (2009, October 7). *The Danger of a Single Story*. TedTalk.

McCraney, T. A. (2010). *The Brother/Sister Plays*. Theatre Communications Group.

Mongeau, L. R. (2010, January 16). *Oakland Tech's Rendition of "Hamlet: Blood in the Brain"*. Oakland North. https://oaklandnorth.net/2010/01/15/oakland-techs-rendition-of-hamlet-blood-in-the-brain-showing-this-weekend/

Montoya, R. J. (2015). *American Night: The Ballad of Juan Jose*. Samuel French.

12

Lineage

Expanding Our Understanding of Identity

The dance of the ancestor is a movement based artistic research practice Jessa works with in order to explore one's ancestry as character work. The first time I experienced it I decided to imagine my grandmother on my father's side who died shortly after I was born. I never met her. As Jessa walked us through a series of questions, I began to explore gestures that my grandmother would have engaged in. It begins by embodying a simple daily task that an ancestor would have participated in. I choose washing dishes and tidying the kitchen. As we went through further prompts to explore and expand the gestures, I found myself enmeshed in a memory that felt real. It felt like time-traveling. The most curious thing about it was that I began to do things with my left hand. And I'm right handed. I later learned that my grandmother was left-handed.

– Mariah

In culturally responsive education through the arts, we place a high value on thinking about the people who came before us, and both the strengths and limitations of their worldviews. It is often the thinking of the people who came before us who can show us who we are and where we are going. Calling on our lineages creates a cultural shift from placing undue high value on individual identity formation and knowledge acquisition to a more interpersonal and collective understanding of the world within our spheres of influence. These spheres do include the self but extend also to the importance of others,

DOI: 10.4324/9781003301226-15

of community, of society, and even to the understanding of one's place within a universal context, or cosmos.

Many educators currently prioritize individual student identity formation and expression, which is a step forward in humanizing the learning experience but still a limited Western/Northern notion of how humans grow. One of the strengths of a global and Indigenous understanding of the self is to recognize the power of the larger "we," an awareness of self in relationship to others, including human and non-human, sentient and nonsentient beings. The "we" is a common worldview found in more collectivist cultures. Lineage amplifies the idea of interconnectedness and interdependence as we co-construct an education that enables us to grapple with contemporary social ills.

It is common practice in many Indigenous cultures to begin a formal introduction of oneself by naming a lineage of teachers, ancestors (human and nonhuman), tribal and cultural affiliations, and of place, including even names of waters and rivers that one is from. One way many teachers have approached this acknowledgement practice with students is through starting a year or a course of study with development of "I am from ..." poems alongside their students.

Youth Speaks executive director and poet Michelle "Mush" Lee practiced this with generations of students and continues to use the form to introduce herself through poetry in a leadership capacity.

> I am a child of South Korean immigrants. I am descended from ancestors with delicate relationships to sound, story, and survival. I am a San Francisco native born inside the belly of the Hip Hop generation. I am a mother and a storyteller. As a young girl, my 할머니 (grandmother) didn't buy Tums or Alka Seltzer when I had a stomach ache, my 할머니 gave me acupuncture with a sewing needle in the living room of her Tenderloin apartment. We didn't buy hamburgers and french fries—we ate lotus root and rice. Like so many of the young writers at Youth Speaks, I, too, have felt neither culturally here nor there. I, too, have felt the loneliness and isolation of being told to exist silently inside the stories of others, and I also know the glory of finding my voice.
>
> – Michelle "Mush" Lee, Executive Director, Youth Speaks

Choosing Lineages

Many humans are born without the knowledge of their genealogy and family histories. Many lineages are painful to excavate. Some stories are too painful or shameful in the retelling. As educators, it is important that we look at our own educational and personal lineages and face them firmly and compassionately, in order that we can be in turn more compassionate with our students' lineages, which likely hold their own complexities.

As artists, we can follow creative lineages that provide techniques, skills, and abilities that help us work with a particular medium or actualize a chosen form of expression. For example, if you are a poet, you likely have knowledge of the poets from the past and present. You likely have studied the shape and sequencing and rhythm of words, the etymology of languages. You have a distinct lineage within the poetry world. You may gravitate to a specific poet and have read everything they've ever written. A lineage like this shapes your thinking and how you craft your own words, your own story. If you play an instrument, your musical lineage consists of the teachers you study with, their cultural heritages, and musicians who compose and play within your genre and even the songs you play.

We can point to lineages that we are drawn to, to better make meaning of who we are and want to be. Appropriation of cultural lineage occurs primarily when there is an absence of authentic or direct connection to the source of that lineage. It also occurs when someone in a dominant caste unassociated with that lineage derives power or profit from the cultural practice. When we find ourselves drawn to a cultural lineage or cultural arts practice that is not our own, or hope to bring a cultural lineage into our classroom, it is useful to call up the concept of "primary source." Is it possible to bring in experts, live or virtual, with a direct lineage to the cultural art you wish to work with? How is the cultural art being held by contemporary artists and local communities from that lineage? Addressing lineage in our lessons leads us to locate and understand our students through their intersectional cultural lenses. Are there intersections in cultural or creative practice that connect to your own lineages and the lineages of your students?

> Lineage relates to narrative in that as an educator I want to invite students to be in touch with their lineages because they're inherently connected with narratives that students hold. In what ways can students reflect on their lineages and be in communication about the importance and impact of them? I invited students to look inward toward their families and backward to where their families are from. Also for the program based on the Universal Declaration of Human Rights, I chose six of them, and I chose rights that seemed like they would be accessible to students particularly in the way they see their own families. Like the right to housing or the right to have a family. What does that mean? I created prompts that ask direct and indirect questions relating to lineage.
>
> – M. Chardiet, Writer and Youth Educator

Lineage and Identity

Much of our attention when it comes to diversity has rested on identity. Teachers have been taught to focus the gaze on the surface of a student's identity and visible social markers rather than looking at the multiple lineages that students hold and how those lineages surface in the context of the classroom. It is not surprising that we have focused on identity rather than lineages, as we live in a society that holds the individual in high esteem. The United States has been categorized as an individualistic culture rather than a collective one in the spectrum of world nation-states. Old narratives like the "rugged individual" and the "isolated genius" have built up the illusion that our identities are separate from our influences. What happens when we allow ourselves to expand the well-intended focus on students' individual identities to include a consideration of multiple lineages? Remember that these lineages might be familial, but they may also be relational, intellectual, creative, or even athletic. Encourage your students to explore lineages that include their heroes and people in history they feel a connection with, along with using their imagination to call on a fictional ancestor they might draw strength from. By invoking lineage in our lessons, there is room to examine and extoll limiting narratives about ourselves and others, and to bring forward connections that expand our sense of identity.

Creative Inquiries
> *How are the connections and relationships between people, ideas, power structures, or knowledge sets through time and place made visible?*
> *Are any harmful lineages in your curriculum possible to identify and interrupt? Are any cultural or cognitive lineages connected to your students' strengths and interests possible to uplift?*

Figure 12.1 Discourse with the ancestors.

Bibliography

Youth Speaks. (2021, November 29). *Meet our New Youth Speaks Executive Director*. https://youthspeaks.org/letter-from-the-ed/

13

Embodiment

Knowledge Made Visible

Embodiment is how we hold and make our learning visible through the body itself. It can be visibly seen, such as a relaxed pose when talking to a colleague, or abrupt energetics held by the body. Embodiment is also invisible but perceived through our actions, decisions, words, rituals, and practices.

Educating is the work of thinking, but we now have scientific evidence (as most cultural traditions have known) that thinking also extends in and through the body. Our bodies are able to perceive and pick up social and environmental patterns and cues around us before our conscious minds do. Our bodies hold and store information, sometimes perceiving the world before we are actively aware. We constantly pick up signifiers on how to engage, interact, and respond through our physical selves and the design of the physical space around us. How does knowledge get held by the body? Can knowledge sets live actively in one's being?

We often discuss how trauma is stored in the body, but joy and connection and positive muscle memory associations can be built up as well, especially in young learners. Through performing arts and physicalized tasks and actions, we can expand our students' opportunities to store and

DOI: 10.4324/9781003301226-16

hold the shapes and patterns of lessons, stories and experiences over time. What we've witnessed is that through embodied practice, we can evolve our minds.

Just as we are mindful of our student's neurodiversity when it comes to planning lessons involving written tasks or mathematical equations, it is important to be aware of modifications and accommodations for tasks that ask for an embodiment of learning. Check in regularly with students as a group and individually on their accessibility needs. We will say, however, that after decades working with students and decades working with adults, it is often the adults who balk most at physicalized or vocalized activities. This makes sense, as our bodies as "elders" have likely had more adverse experiences and potentially developed a more limited range of movement. Students, on the whole, are often liberated by the invitation to engage in embodied learning, in which they can often express expertise, ease, and perhaps even abilities beyond those of their teacher. Especially in linguistically diverse spaces, where literacy tasks are not equally accessible, embodiment as an assessment tool can help students to literally show what they know.

The visual and performing arts in practice are elements that help to bring Gloria Anzaldúa's concept of *conocimiento*, or knowing, alive in the classroom or in any space. The theater and media arts are inherently interdisciplinary forms, where performers, designers, choreographers, writers, directors, and technicians are all in the business of doubling down on metaphors that add complexity to shared understanding.

A sound, lighting, or costume designer's task, for example, is to amplify the themes or throughlines or thoughtlines the ensemble or playwright is exploring. The choreographer likewise is looking to compose a gestural vocabulary that might mirror or purposely clash with the expected aspects of the narrative. Performing arts engage us in practicing how we literally embody knowledge. How can stories be made not only visible, but felt? How might our wisdom be spoken, designed, heard, and moved through space in ways that create meaning and turn wisdom or lines of thought into experiences?

Figure 13.1 The Apollos: Embodied student performance.

What is obviously embodied by the theater arts also applies to any learning space, although it may be less immediately apparent. Elements of design are always present, some intentional, such as the architecture and arrangement of seating, and some unintentional but telling a story about the values and resources in the space nonetheless. Lighting, music, elements of nature, and even works of art or cultural signifiers help our senses to guide us to where our focus is to be placed, often based on where our bodies are in the room.

As we visit varying teachers' classrooms, there are some spaces where the values and ethics are made visible, where the students and teacher are embodying what can sometimes feel comfortably congruent or delightfully incongruent with the rest of a school's culture.

In my own classroom I took up the still highly controversial and sometimes smelly practice of asking students to remove their shoes at the door and proceed to work barefoot or in socks, as I was trained to do in my own lineage of physical theater. Remarkably, after an initial week of balking and making some accommodations where helpful for student comfort and well-being (ordering a few classroom slippers, a large rug, and some natural air freshener as school supplies) the students accepted and even expected this routine. The accompanying physical and vocal warm up that followed upon entry created a ritualized embodiment of learning that definitely altered the space and defined the rest of our time together. Long after I had left the school, my former colleague sent me a communication she had received from her students, upset because a substitute teacher did not respect this class ritual, which had become an embodied tradition. They sent her a video of the rug and the substitute's feet walking in shoes on it and titled it, "Sacrilege!"

– Jessa

While this is an example of literal embodiment practice existing within a dedicated arts classroom environment, often embodiment can be a felt sense of a culture shift in classroom and school cultures. When students embody learning, they take ownership of the lesson as a living, breathing, internal, and external experience.

Creative Inquiries

What might be gained from exploring the knowledge, ideas, and concepts taught in your classroom as physical, emotional, or visible embodied ways of being?

What cultures and wisdoms are already embodied by the teachers and learners in the school community? Can these embodied strengths be mirrored, amplified, expanded?

Figure 13.2 Mariah Rankine-Landers, There's a Twist, 2022.

Bibliography

Anzaldúa, G. E. (2015). *Light in the Dark/Luz en lo Oscuro: Rewriting Identity, Spirituality, Reality* (A. Keating, Ed.). Duke University Press.

Part Four
An Arc of Learning

Part Four:

An Arc of Learning

Figure P4.1 Title page, Part Four: An Arc of Learning.

14

The Art of Praxis

Theory in Practice

Embodying Praxis

It is ironic, but teaching programs don't often teach praxis. So what is praxis, and why do we care? Praxis is a key term that we believe should lead our conversations on education, as it is how we take theory and put it into practice. Praxis is what pedagogy, or a theory of learning, looks like when it is engaged and embodied. It often moves the center of knowledge from the teacher to the learners. Great liberatory educators of our time, in particular Paulo Friere and bell hooks, used this term to help us understand that educational philosophy and educational practice can and should be one and the same. Praxis, at best, is the activation of our values and ethics in our actions as educators. Engaging in praxis looks like enacting methods that are in harmony with your purpose and your intention. Praxis is what our beliefs look like in classroom practice.

A Brief Exercise in Illuminating Praxis

◆ On your own, or ideally in pairs or small groups, select two to three core ethics or values you lead or teach for. Share with another educator in detail. Choose a common value to focus on.
◆ Take turns describing a teaching moment you have led, witnessed, or could imagine that is clearly rooted in this value. What methods and techniques are present? This is an example of praxis.

DOI: 10.4324/9781003301226-18

◆ Select one exemplary moment of praxis from your pair or small group to share with others. Decide an artful way you'd like to share: role play, duet, mini-performance ensemble, etc.
◆ Rehearse and present to the group.
◆ Critically reflect as a community on what values or ethics are apparent in this action.

Creative Inquiries
What elements of praxis are you already doing well?
Has liberation been a felt experience for your learners in real time?
What additions or changes might you make to your lessons in order to lead with praxis at the center of the learning experience?

An Arc of Learning Designed for Educators

It is a gift to be able to share how we have designed our professional development arc of learning with a focus on praxis. Presented here is a researched arc of learning that can help to shift school and learning cultures. Each section focuses on a distinct contemporary artist that we have either been moved to collaborate with in real time or through their creative processes and inquiries from afar. It is an arc of creative practice for social change. In the following chapters we center the creative processes of contemporary artists Adia Millett, Hank Willis Thomas, Amy Sherald, Kerry James Marshall, Anne Bluethenthal, and Anna Deavere Smith. Insights on techniques and methods found in the visual and performing arts model the pedagogical and teaching practices you and your students will benefit from. Moving through each learning session, take note of the introductions to arts and creative practices and see how they might be employed by you in your classroom practice. While you may not use these themes or these artists, these methodologies can be applied right away.

Bibliography

Friere, P. (1970). *Pedagogy of the Oppressed*. Continuum Publishing Corporation.
hooks, b. (2014). *Teaching to Transgress*. Routledge. https://doi.org/10.4324/9780203700280

15

Breaking Patterns

Breaking with Established Norms in Education

"Breaking Patterns" was the name of an exhibit by visual artist Adia Millett, shown to the public at the California African American Museum in Los Angeles in 2019. Like great art can do, I was immediately impacted by the artistry and creative inquiry in the exhibit, which was focused on probing social patterns in the community and how people might break them. As I took in the range of textile work, paintings, and sculptures, I kept thinking about the ways that schools also needed to address the patterns we've been stuck inside of.

– Mariah

DOI: 10.4324/9781003301226-19

Figure 15.1 Adia Millett, "Transition One," 2018, 36″ × 36″, Acrylic on wood.

Engaging with pattern-making is engaging in culture-making. Patterns repeated on a societal scale become culture. As teachers, looking at the cultures of our classrooms and schools helps us in acknowledging the internalized and/or socially expressed patterns we engage in. Upon further inquiry, the courageous teacher starts the process of breaking patterns of harm by asking "How might I unintentionally play out these patterns in my classroom?"

Our brains are pattern seeking machines. Patterns have been mapped in our brains to create shortcuts. We like a shortcut, so that we can offload energy for other functions needed by the body. Healthy habitual patterns help us to engage in the world in productive ways that can be of great benefit. The problem is, we've also mapped shortcuts to navigate the world based on ideas and actions that were programmed unconsciously by the culture that surrounds us, have gone unchecked, that no longer serve us, and that can be harmful.

Many of our societal patterns have their roots in unexamined hierarchies. Based on centuries of unequal power and unchecked beliefs, we exhibit patterns that have become embodied by our very actions, thoughts, and behaviors. We are functioning with ingrained ways of being.

These patterns have been passed down to us like heirlooms. Heirloom patterns often cause us to unconsciously carry out the same function as they did when they were created. They pass along an inherited set of beliefs and values in order to serve a particular set of social functions. In our evolving state of human understanding and growth, it no longer serves us to exist within limiting social patterns connected to an ill-conceived past.

Our patterns, like our lineages, are not binary, and not black and white. They live in a spectrum of colors and shades of gray, needing nuance and subtlety to be accurately assessed. Taking a look at our patterns (personal and collective) allows us to highlight harmful patterns as well as joyous, affirming, and beneficial ones. We can come to recognize that some patterns contain complexity and have been both of service and done damage. For our growth and development as educators, we seek to address the non-working patterns in our lessons, classrooms, and school systems that we wish to see transformed.

Unconscious Versus Conscious Pattern Making

The Harvard Implicit Association Test is a test that helps us to understand the level of unconscious bias in the brain. Every brain contains bias, and these biases are connected to pattern making. Dr. Mazahrin Banaji, a creator of the Implicit Association Test, calls these patterns blindspots. By design, we are unaware of many of the patterns we operate in and through. Social patterns that we grow up inside of largely dictate our participation in the world. Patterns are associated with our societal understanding of identity markers such as gender, age, ability, class, and race. These markers then become the way we participate in the world in our cultural understanding of self and others (Banaji & Greenwald, 2013).

Historian and author Isabel Wilkerson has mapped out how the caste system is a pattern designed and still in operation in the United States context. This caste system pattern categorizes people according to skin color (among other markers) to an assigned hierarchical position in society, generally with white bodied, cis male gendered people at the top. It is a system that was enforced and reinforced through genocide and enslavement beginning in the 1600s (Wilkerson, 2020). This system was perpetuated through laws and policies in the founding of the nation and through reconstruction that limited, restricted, and impeded the liberties of Indigenous and Black people of all genders along with women of all skin tones. Beliefs and values created through this particular caste system have led to patterns of harm that are visibly seen in our schools. Teaching and learning are inscribed with established patterns from the past that continue to shape how we "do" school. These are patterns that we aim to address and break, creating more egalitarian and liberatory patterns for all people in their place.

Internal Patterns in Education

Internal patterns can play out in our lives as belief systems, actions, and ways of being. Internally expressed patterns are patterns we may have learned through our families of origin, cultural interactions, and self-explored ideas and relationships. They are embodied and formed through our engagement and interactions with daily life. For example, a person may have an internally expressed pattern of thinking in which the needs of others come before the needs of the self. This way of thinking would have roots based in the family and culture they grew up in.

A habit is an action that repeats in some form. A habit can become a pattern. Left unchecked, we can develop and participate in habits and patterns that do not serve us. They may cause harm, impede growth, and keep us from participating fully in life. Healthy habits and patterns help us to experience and maintain a higher quality of life.

In education, both internal and externally expressed patterns will impact our classrooms and school cultures. For example, a teacher who externally believes in social justice and breaking patterns of harm may still struggle with some internal patterning of a deficit mindset toward their learners and might unconsciously be playing out old patterns learned through family, culture, or relational contexts.

Social Patterns in Education

A social or socially expressed pattern is often a historical pattern that plays out in today's world. For example, a socially expressed pattern you might find in school might be to force students to walk the perimeter of a playground with their hands behind their backs.

> A school that I taught at for years enforced this practice as a way to get children to "behave." The school was designed to improve the conditions of Black children, having a 98 percent African American/Black identified student demographic. But it did so through a deficit pattern of belief that Black children needed rigorous discipline in order to succeed at school. If they were loud during lunch time, the Dean of Students would make them march silently with their hands behind their backs, restricting them from play or social time with each other. This is a replicated pattern of practice found in incarceration centers and prisons, including the ten-foot chain link fence surrounding the school grounds. This is an example of a socially expressed pattern that needs to be interrupted and recreated. When this happened to my students, I walked outside and told the Dean that he could not do that to them. He insisted he could and that he would write me up for interrupting his behavioral management process. I did what was right and stopped my students in their tracks and said, "We're going inside." I let them have indoor recess and suffered a lengthy conversation with my admin after that. An agreement was reached that I would not interfere with the other classes that were punished this way, but that if I didn't believe my students should walk the fence, I was to collect them and take them inside the classroom for the remainder of their (and my) lunch break.
>
> – Mariah

Socially expressed patterns can become internalized. Internal patterns can become externalized and therefore socially expressed. This cycle can continue in an ongoing loop until it is intentionally broken. Now some might say that this form of strict behavioral conditioning is a form of love, especially in communities where the layers of oppression make it impossible to function in healthy and whole ways. But a liberatory stance asks us to review and let go of ideas that maintain a punitive social order rather than co-create a beautiful one.

Figure 15.2 How many students have you taught to swim against the tide? Image of a Black mermaid drawn by a teacher.

Taking Inventory

We invite you to take an inventory of as many social patterns in place at your school or in your classroom as you can, ones you see as primarily harmful and those that feel liberatory, as well as ones that might be more nuanced and complex. These patterns may also be components of your school or classroom culture, found in routines, practices, rituals, symbols, roles, relationships, resource allocation, celebrations, and so on.

Creative Inquiries
> *What is the origin story of each social pattern you've listed?*
> *Are there external patterns connected to historical harms?*
> *Are there internal patterns associated with teachers and leaders who carry traumas of their own?*
> *Are there patterns that exist with no understanding of how or why?*
> *How are these patterns experienced by the school community? Are they visible or invisible or neutral? Do they feel uplifting? Do they cause harm?*

We have many patterns to break. Looking at the patterns around us will help us identify our most compelling needs and problems, understand them with more clarity, and create new patterns in their place. Once we acknowledge a pattern, we can work to understand it. The process of understanding a pattern can be worked out through cognitive struggle or perhaps more joyously be experienced and understood through art and inquiry.

Working with artist Adia Millett, we discussed how her artistry and inquiry practice of "Breaking Patterns" might be used to accelerate changes in teaching and learning. Adia, open for collaboration, met us for coffee and mapped out how she as a multidisciplinary visual artist explores an idea. Starting with a general concept, she considers materials that make that concept come alive, learning about herself along the way. We discussed what it might feel like to have teachers engage in pattern making, designing a conceptual pattern from their lived experiences, and going through the process of breaking their pattern work and recreating it.

Our first attempt at exploring this concept was with a group of public school educators in Los Angeles. There were a range of educators in the room, from first-year kindergarten instructors to twelfth-grade engineering and science teachers. As we began the process, teachers quietly identified the pattern they wanted to work with. Because we had been working together for some time as a community of practice, there was an established culture of trust in the room. Some sat with very personal patterns, ones they preferred to name only lightly to their colleagues. Others considered patterns playing out in their classroom that they had some responsibility in redesigning. One teacher shared that she had been organizing students based on gender roles and saw that this pattern needed breaking. Another teacher shared how she realized she had restricted learning materials from students simply because she didn't want a messy room. They pieced together fabric and paper to make a collaged image that represented the pattern.

A series of creative inquiries were then introduced as they sat with their art pieces. They quietly scribed in their journals through several prompts that asked them to consider the larger social and internal construction of their pattern.

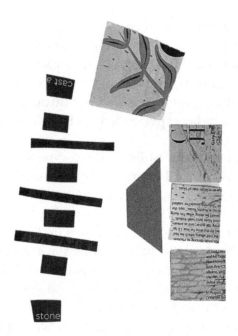

Figure 15.3 Breaking patterns.

When the moment came to "break" their patterns, there was a hush. Nerves rushed forward in the room. "Why the hesitancy?" I thought to myself. I recognized the attachment they were having to what they had created. In a flash I said "Take out your cameras and take a picture of your pattern. This is the hard part. Letting go of something we've been participating in for a long time." Slowly, they began to take apart their patterns. Again a hush fell over the crowd. I noticed how some of them slowly picked up one piece at a time, and others pushed all the pieces of their collage to one side of their studio space to start again. Kenisha, a Black educator, pushed the weight of her body into the back of her chair and sighed. "What is it Kenisha?" I asked. "You know, I'm just realizing that this process is something that I really needed. I think I was aware, but not really, of some of the actions I need to do so I can be more responsive to my students. They are so curious. Why don't I bring that out more in them? Instead I race from subject to subject to get learning objectives done. But is this actually serving them?"

– Mariah

The most fundamental aspect of going through the art-making process is that it surfaces knowledge that cannot be known through cognitive struggle alone. Said another way, allowing yourself to experience art making will illuminate and unlock information pertinent and personal to you.

Monica Sharma, in her book *Radical Transformational Leadership*, calls us to look at visible and invisible patterns for social transformation. She calls for us to see patterns with discernment. Pattern transformation doesn't happen by overcoming it or tolerating it. Transforming inherently involves understanding that a change is taking place. In that change, it becomes our work to make clear and precise choices grounded in values that hold regard for the self and others (Sharma, 2017). Working through patterns creatively may surprise you. The experience can provide the opportunity for observations, reflections, and discernment.

Break and Create

How Can We Break with the Ordinary to Create the Extraordinary?

This design process is geared towards adult learners: teachers and educational practitioners who are ready to make explicit shifts away from harmful patterns of practice into vibrant patterns for social transformation.

Materials:
- A collection of pieces of fabric or paper. Torn bits of a magazine, construction paper, etc.
- A canvas to create on: craft paper, a piece of cardboard, an old cutting board, etc.

Part 1:
1. Gather a selection of the pieces of paper or fabric. A handful of bits of paper or fabric to work with will do.
2. Notice your first impressions about the paper choices you selected. How do the colors or textures speak to you? The sizes?
3. Ask "What pattern do I want to break?" and respond in your journal. Consider either a pattern that you'd like to work on personally, like limiting how much you are on social media, or a pattern that you are curious about in your teaching and learning process (this includes structures, procedures, special design of the classroom, practices, value sets, etc.).
4. Arrange the pieces into an image that represents the pattern. This can be literal or metaphorical. For instance, if you are choosing to work with breaking a pattern of negative self-talk, you might depict an image of a mouth or a face for a literal interpretation, or a depiction of dark clouds might provide a more metaphorical take on the issue.
5. Prepare for reflective writing through responding to a series of questions. This inquiry sequence is connected to visual art making that will expose meaning. The series of questions are adapted from

a framework for narrative intelligence inspired by Erica Williams Simon in her book *You Deserve the Truth: Change the Stories that Shaped Your World and Build a World Changing Life (2020)*.

Identifying Patterns: This first series of questions supports the identification of information surrounding your pattern. Draw, write, or doodle your response to the following questions. There is no "wrong" way to respond.

Creative Inquiries
    What pattern do I want to break?
    What is the origin story of this pattern?
    What do you observe about this pattern?
    What do you think about this pattern?
    What do you wonder about this pattern?
    Look closely at the pattern with a flashlight. What else do you see?
    What story would you be telling if you told this story to a child?

Understanding Patterns: The next series of questions support a deeper understanding of the pattern.

Creative Inquiries
    How do you embody this pattern?
    What purpose does the pattern serve?
    Is the pattern causing pain in any way?
    Is this pattern helping you co-create a world you want to live in?

Figure 15.4 Heart pattern.

Part 2: **Creating Patterns:** Create a New Pattern

1. Stretch, have some water, and tend to your body. Thinking through patterns takes energy. Reset the nervous system and mind so that you do not stay stuck in a space that you are wrestling with for too long.
2. Before moving on, consider taking a photo of your pattern. If you feel in love with your art piece, it can be difficult to let it go. Through documentation, you can have a record of what it looked like.
3. Break your pattern. Create a new pattern. Change and rearrange the pieces in some way. Pause and reflect on how you broke it apart. Did you move all the pieces off the canvas swiftly? Did you stop and look at it first and then make an artistic choice to move one piece at a time? This is good metaphorical information that may be reflective of how we individually go about breaking or changing social or internal patterns or shifting a habit in our day-to-day lives.
4. Journal your response, through words or drawings, to this next set of inquiries as you think about how to go about creating something new.

Creative Inquiries
What if you created something new?
Are you able to feel radiant inside this new pattern or design?
Could this way of being alter the direction of your life?
Could it be a part of a personal or collective healing?

---

5. If you are working with others, create a reflective experience for you and your colleagues to share the process of breaking and creating patterns. In this space for sharing, encourage sharing only that which feels safe and useful to share about the insights that were made and connections that were established. A few formats that support a reflective process are as follows:
    o   Story Circle: Each person has 1–2 uninterrupted minutes to share their work and insights.
    o   Gallery: Invite each person to write an artist statement for their work. Place art pieces around the room as a curator would place art in a gallery. Walk around the room and view the art, engaging with the artist statements and speaking with others about what you see.
    o   Chalk Talk: Write collectively on a large sheet of paper (we like to cover tables with craft paper) and have each person write

reflective statements. As you write, pause to read the reflections of others and respond in kind to what others have written down, via written commentary.

Intellectually being able to identify the patterns we wish to change is something most people can want to do, but don't necessarily take action on. Working through an artistic research process can expand our ability to receive new information, develop better clarity, and provide actionable steps that we can take to make changes. It gives us the distance and even playfulness that might be required to more accurately observe a pattern's origins and apply novel solutions.

We don't live a life, we live a pattern. Who is going to be the pattern disruptor?

– Dr. Shefali Tsabary, Clinical Psychologist

Critical Reflections
What might happen when we start to see, break, and create new social patterns from those long held within teaching and learning?
What arts medium might I explore more deeply (visual art making, writing and storytelling, music) to activate meaning making and to explore unconscious biases that have been built into my classroom practices and teacher approach?

Bibliography

Banaji, M. R., & Greenwald, A. G. (2013). *Blindspot: Hidden Biases of Good People*. Random House.

Sharma, M. (2017). *Radical Transformational Leadership: Strategic Action for Change Agents*. North Atlantic Books.

Wilkerson, I. (2020). *Caste: The Origins of Our Discontents*. Random House.

Williams Simon, E. (2020). *You Deserve the Truth: Change the Stories that Shaped your World and Build a World Changing Life*. Gallery.

16

Culture, Cognition, and the Arts
Using Creativity to Think Expansively

Culture, cognition, and the arts are a braiding of three components that can be considered as mutually dependent in producing schools that love our students.

Culture

> Culture, like food, is necessary to sustain us. It molds us and shapes our relations to each other. An inequitable culture is one in which people do not have the same power to create, access, or circulate their practices, works, ideas and stories. It is one in which people cannot represent themselves equally. To say that American culture is inequitable is to say that it moves us away from seeing each other in our full humanity. It is to say that the culture does not paint a more just society.
>
> – Jeff Chang, Writer/Cultural Strategist

Culture is a flexible container through which we participate and engage with the world. Culture dictates our belief systems, mindsets, behaviors, and perceptions. We are not easily able to separate ourselves from culture. It is both tangible and intangible, like the air we breathe. When we become more

DOI: 10.4324/9781003301226-20

intentional around not only incorporating but building and transforming culture, we can more easily actualize a theoretical concept like a pedagogy of love.

Cognition

> Human minds have invented not one cognitive universe, but 7,000—there are 7,000 languages spoken around the world. And we can create many more. Languages, of course, are living things, things that we can hone and change to suit our needs … right now, almost everything we know about the human mind and human brain is based on studies of usually American English-speaking undergraduates at universities. That excludes almost all humans. Right? So what we know about the human mind is actually incredibly narrow and biased, and our science has to do better.
>
> – Dr. Lera Boroditsky, Cognitive Scientist

Cognition is thinking. Education in our time has shifted. We are in a time where information is readily available but the critical thinking skills needed to process and integrate that information need focus and support. Ideally, we are no longer teaching only subjects; we are teaching thinking about thinking. How cultures often do that is through the performing, visual, media, and language arts.

The Program for International Student Assessment (PISA) report from 2018 showed that over 10 million students in the United States could not perform the most basic reading skills, and only 1 in 10 children were able to tell the difference between fact and fiction. The report showed that there has been no improvement in learning outcomes over the last decade, even though spending on students has gone up by 15 percent. In 2022 the PISA report added creative thinking as a category for assessment. This decision reflects a prioritization of creative practice in education as the world moves into a conceptual era. Each of us has a renewed purpose to teach creative thinking skills in order to grow learners' capacity to think critically and metacognitively.

Arts

The arts are powerful levers that shift culture and consciousness. The arts are avenues for cultural belonging, self-expression, and in-depth thinking. All applied practices of creative thought may be considered artful. If we think metaphorically of culture as the air that surrounds us, then the imagination, art, and creativity might be thought of as the atoms and molecules that make up our cultural air. Much of cultural development can be traced to creative responses to environmental stimuli. These "art atoms" are the binding elements through which we come to know ourselves, each other, and the world. The arts activate and use our spectrum of senses to expand and evolve our thinking, and grow our conscious awareness as we deepen our connection and knowledge of the world around us. Our friends at the Center for Cultural Power have studied this phenomenon and make a compelling argument that culture in turn transforms our societal belief systems faster than policies or economics.

There is an interconnected relationship between art, culture, and cognition that is central to the design of lessons that love our students. As we pay attention to the past, we can be better informed about our current state of affairs and by default the sometimes unchecked historical patterns and systems that are repeating themselves in new forms. Doing so will help us bridge from a caste-based culture to a culture of belonging. The thinking we need for this cultural leap requires tacit knowledge, which comes from learning spaces where we are engaged with one another. This type of thinking happens naturally when we shift away from a banking method of teaching or regurgitation of canned curriculum. Trying to deposit content knowledge into students is a fruitless task.

Culture, cognition, and the arts, once embodied, can begin to work in harmony with each other as we plan and develop lessons, procedures, and curricula that will love our children. Understanding how they intersect will deepen your expertise in how you design your lessons.

> Because race is someone else's fantasy. It's someone else's fiction. This idea that people are born with these dominant, innate characteristics that dictate by the millions is absurd. It's comical. It's ridiculous, yet and still, it's been so ingrained in me to code these people—even coding you by the wisp in your hair, the thickness of your eyebrows, the tone of your skin in summer.
>
> – Hank Willis Thomas, Contemporary Artist

In the spring of 2012, I was introduced to the work of Hank Willis Thomas. Captivated by his piece *The Cotton Bowl*, I realized it could help communicate living systems in education that need our attention. It is an image of two Black bodied men face to face in a crouched position. One man seemingly is picking cotton in a field, wearing overalls, his face covered by a wide brim straw hat. The other man wears a football uniform with his hand on the yardline of a football field. The backdrop is all black. The juxtaposition unnerved me immediately. How clearly Hank was able to tell a story of lineage, narrative, power and embodiment all in one frame. The image outlined a system of oppression, with a clear visual of how one system evolved into a similar system, mirrored in a contemporary form.

– Mariah

Figure 16.1 *Hank Willis Thomas, The Cotton Bowl, 2011 digital c-print 50 x 73 inches.*
© Hank Willis Thomas Courtesy of the artist and Jack Shainman Gallery, New York.

We knew that this image would serve to help educators discuss concepts of power in education, systems of inequity, and the perpetuated harms that remain in place inside our schools. We also knew that we could exemplify how to create a culture of thinking and teach core elements of lesson design that utilize the role of culture, cognition and the arts.

Our first attempt was for a group of educators in Eugene, Oregon— a largely white bodied group of teachers and artists. I introduced my favorite thinking routine from Agency by Design: parts, purposes, and complexities. It is a thinking routine that supports critical thought around systems, be they social or mechanical. It remains one of my preferred protocols to use for transformational thinking. When I put the image on the screen I knew I had to give the audience a second to register what they were looking at. It can be jarring to see. This is the power of art.

I asked the group to name and list the parts that they saw. Then they listed the purposes to each part that they saw. Then they wrote down what *felt* complex or what *was* complex about the image. A discussion ensued about the parts and purposes of education and the complexities that we are dealing with today. Remarks were made about race, power, repeated systems of harm, white supremacy, replicated patterns in education, racialized experiences, and social hierarchies. Some brought up historical facts that added to the collective learning. After a lengthy discussion, I asked them to stand up and face a partner.

I began by having the teachers stand face to face and to begin mirroring each other. Person A and Person B each took a turn leading soft and easy gestures to be mirrored back to them. Then I had the audience practice looking into each other's eyes for half a minute. "Shake it out," I said. This allowed for a restart. This time I asked them each to assume the stance from one of the figures in the image. Person A was to be the person picking cotton, and Person B was to be the football player. They crouched down into the three point stance. The room was silent. Bodies that needed adjustments sat in a chair while resuming the rest of the pose. Some could only bend slightly forward. I asked them to look into each other's eyes. Silently they held the gaze of the person in front of them. Then I invited Person A to repeat after me in a whisper, "I am your past. What things have changed? What things remain the same?" Next I invited Person B to repeat after me in a whisper, "I am your future. What things have changed? What things remain the same?" I counted to ten inside my head. You could hear a pin drop. "Release, and let it go." They shook out the stance and returned to a standing position with their partner. I could see tears streaming down several faces. I asked them to thank their partner. Some hugs ensued before everyone took their place. They took a minute to journal before we proceed any further.

The next opportunity to lead this lesson was in Los Angeles. This time there were a handful of Black male PE teachers in the room. Two of them were football coaches. Upon seeing the image, they resisted it. They offered commentary about how good the sport was for students of color during the thinking routine, until they got into the poses and worked through the gestures. When we broke the silence that we held after speaking the dialogue, one teacher spoke and said, "To be honest this has me thinking really deep. Football is something I've loved my whole life, and I'm not leaving it, but I am realizing how inequitable the system is. You know, most of the owners of these football leagues are white men? And most of the money goes to the league and these white owners. I'm honestly shook because I don't know what to do now." Another teacher spoke up and said, "I think we look into co-ownership. And teach our young athletes how to manage their money and not be had." The conversation expanded to include considering the various systems designed for and through the enslavement and exploitation of Black and Indigenous peoples and what their contemporary design was. The more things change, the more things stay the same.

– Mariah

What Things Remain the Same?

Addressing power structures held in our schools and classrooms is ongoing work until we arrive at a location of wellness. *The Cotton Bowl* teaches us that the past is not past at all, but lives on as patterns, behaviors, systems and structures. If you are teaching in a learning culture stuck in a default operating system of the past, address it. If you're leading a school stuck in an old paradigm, illuminating the connections between past and present systems can be a hard task to achieve. We have been poised to understand and build towards equity in education, but are we prepared to consider the contemporary restructuring of old societal frames?

> The function of art has always been to break through the crust of conventionalized and routine consciousness.
>
> – John Dewey, Educational Reformer

The Past Stares into the Future

What does *The Cotton Bowl* have to teach us about lessons that love our students? *The Cotton Bowl* can help us explore how we practice building cultures of care and cultures of thinking inside schools. It can help us examine racialized experiences, practices, patterns, and systems that remain embedded in our landscape. When we allow ourselves to see our humanity and current conditions through a historical lens, we can begin to repair the damage caused by hegemonic teaching methodologies based in domination over students.

Get Situated: Humanizing Methodologies

The following are a few key methodologies that you can employ as you embark on creating lessons designed with a standard of love. When we work with Hank's image of *The Cotton Bowl*, we introduce the following concepts. They are methods of pedagogical practice that can be applied to any lesson in any discipline in developmentally thoughtful ways.

Pathways of Engagement

What are commonly referred to as norms or agreements we like to call pathways of engagement. In a pathway of engagement, we are provided guidelines for what might be experienced when working with high-intensity concepts, particularly in groups that have diverse knowledge sets regarding history and a range of understandings of the systems and structures around us. We suggest that you take a moment to discuss the following key ideas when working with complex subject matter in a mixed crowd of learners.

- ◆ Acknowledge that exploring heavy topics through an embodied practice can bring up strong reactions and emotions. Enter in a way that feels generative and kind, and pause for self-care as needed. When discomfort arises, never force a person to experience the pain. We are not seeking to press further on an open wound. We are seeking a creative process for research, which can be healing.
- ◆ Shift systemic and unequal power structures in real time. Center the words, voices, and experiences of those closest to the pain and honor the wisdom of embodied expertise. For example, if you are invoking *The Cotton Bowl* image with adult learners, flip the script to honor, center, and consider the perspectives of those most impacted by structural anti-Black racism in particular, as this art piece hones in on generational trauma on Black bodies.
- ◆ Invite participants who are closest to the pain to reframe publicly or privately as they wish. Processing pain in a mixed identity crowd can come with discomfort. For this reason it can be supportive to set up an expectation for limited cross talk. Using a thinking routine can support this.

Connection

Lessons that love our students are grounded in the knowledge that trusting, healthy, and safe relationships are key to courage, transformation and growth. Culturally responsive pedagogy prioritizes caring relationships with students and families as a driver in accelerating learning outcomes.

Many people of the global majority hail from a lineage of collectivist cultures where relationships are more obviously foundational to survival and community life. It is no less important to our contemporary students' survival that they build connection and relationship in our classrooms and communities in a U.S. cultural context today.

Eye Contact

In the theater arts, eye contact is an essential skill to practice in order to deepen relationships with scene partners. When practiced at length, it stimulates connection and can even produce feelings of love. For this reason, a practice of eye contact is one way to develop connection in the classroom. For some, the practice of making eye contact can be unnerving, and there are cultural differences around the use of eye contact as a sign of respect and/or disrespect. Making eye contact can also cause stress for some neurodiverse learners. If there are cultural or personal barriers you anticipate with your students, you can practice simply being mutually observant and present instead. Invite participants to notice the presence of the person standing in front of them. Their eyes can gaze at the person's feet, at the top of the head, or remain closed. See if you can practice eye contact or mutual observation for at least one minute. Stretch to longer amounts as trust builds over time.

The Profound Role of Gesture and Movement in Thinking

Movement supports the encoding process, the work of the brain to store and organize information for later retrieval. It's hard to conceptualize, but it is true: thinking takes place beyond our brain. It is also true that the more we move, the better we will think (Murphy Paul, 2021).

Gestures are a simple yet complex way that the body expresses thought and meaning. Fundamentally, gestures communicate information in multiple ways that can reach learners across the many barriers of language. Most researchers will name that up to 93 percent of communication is nonverbal.

In working with movement, we acknowledge that we are all in different bodies with differing abilities, so throughout your own practice we invite you to engage as works best for your own body, adjusting as needed.

Socially Distributed Cognition: Think Together

Humans are wired to connect with each other and are highly interdependent social creatures, dependent on others for our well-being. Even the lone wolf concept of the solitary genius is a myth. Creating a culture of care involves creating more ways that we can think together. Students have the potential to expand thinking abilities through witnessing one another's movements and gestures. Synchronous movements in particular are associated with socially distributed cognition, or thinking together.

Practicing gestures and movements as an ensemble helps learners to develop collaborative relationships and signals to the group that we are willing to observe and reflect others to achieve a shared goal or idea, and it tells our brains that we are safe to learn something new. In forming stronger bonds as a classroom or school culture and creating meaningful cultures of care, shared movement is a useful practice. As artists and learners, exploring gestures and movement can often help us to connect ideas and information in new ways.

Collaborative Stretch

Use collaborative stretches as a way to warm up and share leadership and power actively with any group. Be certain to invite people to engage as their own bodies and ranges of motion will allow, acknowledging differing abilities while pressing folks to take a healthy risk. Adults, having spent more time in their bodies, often have more limitations or held trauma than students, who need access to movement in order to process and retain information. Begin with one learner, and have them lead a basic stretch for the group. The group then engages in the stretch. Pass the leadership along until everyone has led a stretch.

Students who have neurodiversity or trauma responses may often find movement, gesture, and embodied learning styles especially useful in encoding learning and expressing understanding, as long as it is held within a culture of consent. The student who struggles with the inhumane task of sitting still at a desk for many hours a day may find great freedom in using movement to express thought. Here Universal Design principles are useful. What is good for a targeted subset of students is generally beneficial to whole group learning styles.

Mirroring

When mirroring another person, you are activating mirror neurons. Mirror neurons are what help us to understand the meaning of an action and are a core layer of building empathy. Our gestures can actually shift our emotional state; for example, taking on a power pose can indeed help us to feel more powerful. The practice of mirroring can start to deepen connections between learners and support the creation of a culture of belonging.

To practice mirroring, have learners stand face to face with each other. Pairs should select who will lead first and who will lead second. (This is a great time to practice flipping the script). Person A should start out with small gestures like raising an arm slowly and then build to more whole-body movements. Partner B will mirror as though they are the mirror reflection of person A. Switch leads after a minute or so.

Mirror, Don't Mimic

Reflecting a person's words, phrases, and/or movements as a performing artist is a gift, and should not attempt to mimic or mock but instead to find a point of authentic connection between two separate individuals. Social power dynamics are always at play when mirroring or portraying another human being. The invitation is to find connection while respecting difference, done with consent and the intention of witnessing, honoring, and empathizing with someone's way of speaking and moving through the world. Feeling heard and seen is a human need that supports the culture of care you are developing.

Flocking

Explore the ways birds move together. They flock. They take turns becoming the lead, which requires the birds to take note of where the lead shifted to. You can practice this with students by standing together in a huddle or at their desks. Have everyone face in one direction and select someone to start off a series of movements to be mirrored by the rest of the group. After 30 seconds or so, the leader should hand off leading the group to someone nearby using eye contact or a simple gesture. The practice continues until everyone has had a chance to lead. Students will have the opportunity to engage with both divergent and convergent creative thinking. Note that your students may use abstract creative gestures, or they may want to flock in a style more akin to popular cultural references. We advocate following the lead of your students and also inviting them to create something new. Flocking is not so much how you practice synchronicity, but stretching into the concept of shared leadership and whole body expression and listening that matters most.

Use a Thinking Routine to Increase Cognition

Remember that a thinking routine is a flexible tool for critical thinking. We use thinking routines to assist the brain in meaning making and creativity. Here is how we have used the thinking routine from our friends at Agency by Design called 'Parts, Purposes and Complexities' to look at Hank Willis Thomas's work.

Go back and look at the image.

◆ Parts
   ○ While looking at the image, write down all the parts that you see. Be very specific, such as, "I see a silver helmet," or "I see cotton blooms," or "I see a white line." Take a moment to write down each of the parts you see.
◆ Purposes
   ○ Now, looking at the list you have in front of you, list the purposes of each part. For instance, "The purpose of the silver helmet is to keep the person's head safe." "The purpose of the dirt is to grow cotton." Take a moment to list out the purposes apparent to you.
◆ Complexities
   ○ This image is titled *The Cotton Bowl*. The name itself implies complexity. This part of the routine is where we will describe what looks or feels complex about this image. You can use inference here to derive meaning from the image. You can also speculate based on your own history, knowledge, and lived experience. Go ahead and do a free write about how this image holds complexity for you.

Critical Reflections
   Where might I expand my use of creative dialogue, gesture, and character development to help students embody learning and create cultures of thinking?
   How might the use of thinking routines in my classroom be offered as an initial engagement into metacognition?

Bibliography

Boroditsky, L. (2018) *How Language Shapes the Way We Think*. TED Talk.
Chang, J. (2016). *We Gon' Be Alright: Notes on Race and Resegregation*. Picador.
Dewey, J. (2016). *The Public and It's Problems: An Essay in Political Inquiry*. (M. L. Rogers, Ed.). Swallow Press.

LOOKING CLOSELY. (n.d.). Parts, Purposes, Complexities. Agency by Design | www.agencybydesign.org Project Zero | Harvard Graduate School of Education http://www.pz.harvard.edu/sites/default/files/AbD_PPC.pdf

Organization for Economic Cooperation and Development. (n.d.). *PISA Report*. https://www.oecd.org/pisa/

The Ideaspace. (2021). Artist Hank Willis Thomas on Playing Infinite Games. https://ideaspace.substack.com/p/artist-hank-willis-thomas-on-playing

17

Grayscale

Deepening Wisdom Around Racialized Experiences

Figure 17.1 Grayscale. Artwork by (T)sedey Gebreyes, Untitled, Grayscale Workshop, MOAD 2021.

DOI: 10.4324/9781003301226-21

Do you have a racialized "American" identity? How would you describe it? Journalist Michele Norris invites her audiences to scribe a six word racialized biography in her Race Card Project. This creative prompt asks us to summarize our identities through our racialized experiences that contain interconnected and disconnected stories about who we are and how we are perceived. Michele's prompt helps us see that everyone has a racialized "American" story to tell. We have all been racialized.

Race is a social construct. As devised and characterized by anthropologist Carl Linneaus (1707–1778), skin color became a way to identify and classify humans (Sussman, 2016). The extension of his faulty notions of race had devastating consequences—consequences that are ongoing, far reaching, and at the root of genocides around the world. These are consequences that are felt and played out in our system of education.

Before Linneaus, twenty African people in 1619 were brought to the North American shores to be sold to the English colony that had settled there. Prior to that, in 1455 and again in 1492, a papal bull named the Doctrine of Discovery was signed stating that any land not inhabited by Christians was available to be discovered, claimed, and exploited. Historian Roxanne Dunbar-Ortiz, author of *An Indigenous People's History of the United States*, graciously spent time with us when we developed our *Rise Up! An American Curriculum*. Roxanne looked us in the eye and told us point blank that it was a misconception that Hamilton was an immigrant. Hamilton's move to the new colony was merely a sanctioned transfer. Dunbar-Ortiz reminded us about the centuries old Doctrine of Discovery, a papal bull that gave permission to Europeans to discover, seize, and claim right to lands they encountered (2015). It was not until March of 2023 that the Vatican finally denounced the Doctrine.

This Doctrine of Discovery was used to create a structure to sanctify the oppression and erasure of people whom European imperialists encountered. Internal and external patterns of dominance were established which led to the creation of a caste system through the fiction of a racialized "white" morally superior human, and all others. European American settler colonists enslaved 12.5 million Africans, and it is estimated that 2 million did not survive the middle passage. It is also estimated that the Indigenous population of the Americas was decimated by the genocide of 100 million people (Ortiz, 2015).

How might our relationships be different if racialization was not created and systemically embedded within cultures and structures? How has racialization through settler colonization impacted our school system at large? The creation of the idea of race has done real damage to the planet. Exploring grayscale can help us wrestle with ideas of the construction of racialized identities so that healing can occur.

When we moved to Baton Rouge, Louisiana for a brief time when I was eight years old, I learned firsthand just how deeply racism and segregation still existed in the United States. Instantaneously and simultaneously I understood that I could not escape my whiteness, and that it came with a strange undeserved educational privilege in particular. My first day at public school, the students and teachers were all Black and the principal was white. I recall no books and few resources in the fourth-grade classroom, beyond the chalkboard and desks, pencils and lined paper, and many of the students had not yet been taught to read. The class structure was punitive and discipline based. I was swiftly sent to the principal's office for non-compliance … "wasting" paper by doodling on it (something as an artist's daughter I had no comprehension of), as well as not knowing to call the teacher "ma'am" as a California kid, and therefore inadvertently disrespecting her deeply. The principal suggested to my mother that I be held out of school, since I could already read beyond grade level (thank you Mama and *Sesame Street*). There was a clear non-spoken agenda that was likely more significant, which was that I did not belong there racially. A few students had been calling me names and there was some physical bullying, so I did learn to empathize around race-based harm, through my very temporary interpersonal experience of minority status. This is not to say I believe, then or now, that reverse structural racism is a thing.

I was pulled from the school, and I know now that my grandfather sent just enough money so that I could enroll in a private school (an example of comparative white generational wealth, even though I had always considered my mom and I as in the "starving artist" lower middle class) where I noticed immediately that the only Black person there was the custodian. The reality of the second school was an equally shocking experience, and I can't say I recall the education itself being any stronger, although the resources were more abundant. While there, none of the white kids were allowed into my home, mostly because I had a single mother, did not go to church, and lived in what I was told later was a rare mixed race "poor" neighborhood of Baton Rouge in 1984. I felt immobilizing shame and confusion around my outsider status, my whiteness, my comparative privilege, comparative poverty, and the stark inequities I was seeing first hand, but I had no words or names for these feelings. Although I hailed from a family of courageous multi-generational race-conscious social activists, I do not recall anyone discussing any of the interpersonal racial realities of this time with me. For my ninth birthday, my mom gave me the great gift of bringing me to a Cyndi Lauper concert in New Orleans. Cyndi dedicated the concert to her favorite character, Celie, from Alice Walker's relatively new novel *The Color Purple*. Voracious reader and fan that I was, I followed Cyndi's advice and read Walker's novel that year … getting complex contexts on race (And life! And womanhood!) I was only beginning to comprehend. Later in my early 20s, at a talk and book signing, I nervously and awkwardly said to Ms. Walker, "I believe you saved my life." She looked at my still-blonde self skeptically, but graciously signed.

– Jessa

Laws to prevent access to educational opportunities have been at the root cause of inequitable educational outcomes. Laws such as Prop 13 from 1976 in the state of California set up a system of unequal finances to support schools. Property taxes began to go directly to the schools in that area, instead of being used as shared resources. There are many laws and policies that have served the purpose of exclusion, dominance, and oppression in our school system. State and local policies often create an "our children versus their children" mentality. As you look around at your own school site, you may see the outcomes of a system of social power that began centuries ago.

Intersectionality

Using grayscale as a modality to understand and rethink our perceptions of race and identity allows for a fuller perspective. It helps us to process falsehoods and truths that have shaped our understanding of ourselves. It offers critical reflection of where and who we might evolve into, particularly for our students who recognize that our past ideas are not sufficient for the world they are experiencing, and conceiving of, for their future.

To ignore that race is ever present is to ignore and deny humanity the chance to change and heal. Race as a social construct means that we can rethink the concept in the same way that we are rethinking gender (because gender is also a social construct). For this reason, we work with Amy Sherald's artistic inquiry around "Grayscale."

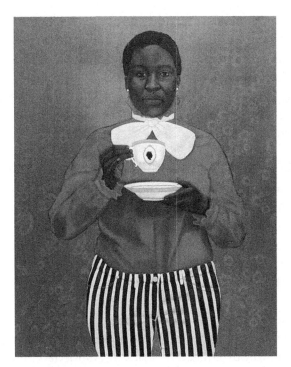

Figure 17.2 Amy Sherald, *Grand Dame Queenie*, 2012, oil on canvas, 54″ × 43″ (137.2 × 109.2 cm).

© Amy Sherald. Courtesy the artist and Hauser & Wirth.

Exploring Grayscale

Amy Sherald is the artist who painted Michelle Obama's portrait in 2018. Amy uses grayscale as a central concept in her work as a way to support audiences to rethink race.

Amy's process and inquiry into grayscale has led us into a literal and metaphorical exploration with educators. Sherald uses the colors Naples Yellow and Mars Black to create hues of gray that depict skin tones of Black and African American peoples. Grayscale is a term in visual arts used to speak of the wide range of gray found in the spectrum between black and white. The idea of grayscale is shared metaphorically to say that we are more than the confines of a caste system that dictates where we belong and who we belong with. Grayscale can be a metaphorical representation of intersections of identity and lineage, representing the creation of more complex and truthful narratives.

Our first experience of leading the ideas of grayscale to explore our racialized identities was at Stanford University. Participants were led through the creation of abstract contour drawings with a partner. They then shaded their images with a pencil to create a grayscale look. Using a modified 3-2-1 Bridge

Thinking routine, they considered ideas, questions, and metaphorical thinking about their racialized identity within a U.S. context.

Grayscale allows for what is complex to be seen, understood, and acknowledged just as it is. It complicates the single story narrative of race, identity, and the stories that make up our perspectives. These narratives play out in how we teach, how we design our lessons, how we assess, and how we move through the school day.

> How are the intersectional identities of the educators, students, families, and communities at your school site a visible or invisible part of the school culture and curriculum?

The untangling of narratives is not meant to provide respite from the work of discussing race in education but to allow for a more profound way to see the impacts of its entanglement.

Practicing Grayscale

Our friend and mentor, artist Susan Wolf, brought forward the practice of blind contour drawings in our collective work at Alameda County Office of Education from 2014 to 2018. Her intention was to introduce drawing to educators who had little arts education experiences in their own K–12 and collegiate training. Susan first instructed on what a blind contour drawing is: depicting a person, place, or thing through the act of drawing it without looking at your hand or paper. You try not to pick up your pencil, and make one continuous line containing all the shapes and details you can manage to depict through close observation. The outcome looks something like the accompanying figure.

Figure 17.3 Abstract contour drawing.

In practicing blind contour drawings, we have taken to calling them abstract contour drawings so as to not perpetuate ableist language.

Abstract Contour Drawing

Sit face to face and create an abstract contour drawing of a partner. Start at the top of the head and move down to create the shape of the face. Follow the lines and contours of the face, allowing your hand to cross back over lines to make details found in the facial structure. Remember, don't pick up your hand and don't look at your work while you draw!

Likely you and your partner will have a great laugh and some commentary to share about how it felt to draw each other in this way. What did it require of you to create a drawing? What did it feel like to look at an image drawn abstractly in your likeness? See if you can recognize the studio habits of mind in your attempts to create: Did you observe, reflect, stretch and explore, express, engage and persist, understand the (art) world, develop craft, envision? Don't forget our addition of risk! Where did you take an artistic risk?

Paint

If you are working in pairs, trade art pieces so that you can work with an image of yourself. You can also make an abstract painting of yourself using a mirror or a photo to create an image to work with for the next steps.

Using watercolors or gouache paints, explore using grayscale to color in your image. Amy Sherald uses Mars Black and Naples Yellow (you can find these if you are using gouache paint). If you are using watercolors, use yellow and black. Explore mixing different amounts of each color together to get to a shade that you'd like to work with. You can explore different shading techniques using lighter grayscale in certain parts of the image and darker shades in other parts of it.

If you find yourself unable to accurately depict your skin tone with the colors at hand, we invite you to sit with this experience and any frustrations around representation that may arise for you. If you are within a dominant racialized caste, you may not have had this experience prior to this moment. This can help to increase empathy for the experience of not being accurately represented or having access to products in your skin tone that people with darker skin tones experience regularly.

Figure 17.4 Grayscale drawing by participant.

Asking the Hard Questions

To further work with grayscale, excavate some narratives and expand your current perspectives. In a journal, or adding text to the image you've made, respond to the following series of questions:

- What is the story of your racialized "American" identity?
- How is your racialized identity playing out in your life, your school, and inside your classroom? It can be difficult to acknowledge some of the ways a racialized identity plays out, but the insight will usually outweigh momentary discomfort.
- Consider which dominant narratives are in the background. There has been a construction of the "American" story that in the U.S. we are all living in. These narratives may serve some but may not serve others in the same way. For example, one dominant narrative is the standard of a heteronormative nuclear family structure. Another is the myth of the Model Minority stereotype applied to only certain groups of immigrants in particular. Think of a dominant narrative

that has not served you or your students well. For example, the narrative that students who speak more than one language have deficits rather than strengths, or the narrative that test scores indicate intelligence.

- Stop and reflect. Develop this narrative into a more complex and truthful narrative that better serves you and your students. Evolve or expand the narrative. Example: Intelligence is more than we've been told. Test scores are being deemed less essential to success and college admissions. Being multilingual has been shown to have significant cognitive benefits. What then is intelligence? Is it time we rely less on standards of intelligence devised by one particular caste or dominant group within a U.S. context?

The LOVE Protocol

L.O.V.E.

WHAT DO YOU **LOVE** ABOUT YOUR IMAGE/ARTWORK?

WHAT DO YOU **OBSERVE** ABOUT YOUR WORK? CONSIDER OBSERVATIONS ABOUT PROCESS, IDEAS AND INSIGHTS WHILE MAKING YOUR ART.

WHAT DO YOU **VALUE** ABOUT YOUR WORK?

WHAT WOULD YOU **EXPAND** UPON IN YOUR WORK? WHERE WOULD YOU EVOLVE AN IDEA OR THE ART ITSELF?

Figure 17.5 The LOVE Protocol questions for grayscale.

After creating an image of the self using grayscale and walking through ideas, questions, and metaphors about one's racialized experience, use the LOVE Protocol to deepen your metacognition and artistic process.

Love Letter

Take a moment to write yourself a love letter that honors who you are, where you come from, and where you're going. Be honest with yourself about the many parts of your racialized U.S. identity. What is there to love? Is there anything that needs to be reexamined, remixed, or released? What comprises your grayscale life?

Creative Inquiries

What was of value for you in considering the story of your societal and personal racialized identities?

What caused discomfort and how did you move through?

Through artistic exploration, how might the concept of grayscale inform your own culturally responsive teaching and learning practice?

Bibliography

Dunbar-Ortiz, R. (2015). *An Indigenous Peoples' History of the United States*. Beacon Press.

Hauser & Wirth. (n.d.). *Amy Sherald – Hauser & Wirth*. https://www.hauserwirth.com/artists/11577-amy-sherald/

Michele Norris. (2012, March 10). The Race Card Project. https://theracecardproject.com/michele-norris/

Sussman, R. W. (2016). *The Myth of Race: The Troubling Persistence of an Unscientific Idea*. Harvard University Press.

18

Heirlooms and Accessories
Facing Historical Truths and Practicing Repair

In the art piece entitled *Heirlooms and Accessories*, artist Kerry James Marshall describes the visual composition and rendering of a lynching that took place in Indiana in 1930. Using Lawrence Beitler's 1930 photograph of the murders of Thomas Shipp and Abram Smith, Kerry interrogates the legacy of racial violence. He focuses the gaze of the viewer on three white bodied women whose faces are turned to the camera at the point it was taken. Kerry forces the viewer to contend with the participants in the lynching rather than on the direct violence of the lynching itself. The image asks you to look at the formation of white immunity and connect the dots between history, legacy, and the current moment.

> I encountered *Heirlooms and Accessories* first hand on a trip to see the extraordinary Kerry James Marshall's thirty-five-year retrospective exhibition. I was unprepared for the encounter. Immensely enjoying the vibrant depictions of Black bodied people defying the circumstances of racism and going on about their business as humans, it was an absolute jolt to my system to turn into the room that held *Heirlooms and Accessories*. I spotted it from across the room, a series of three panels all in white, framed in white, hanging side by side. At first glance, that was all I could see. White images with three faces. One singular face highlighted in each image. Immediately I felt disturbed. As I walked closer to the images and began to make out what I was seeing, I stood aghast. I was looking at the murder as described above, of two Black men.
>
> – Mariah

DOI: 10.4324/9781003301226-22

Figure 18.1 Kerry James Marshall Heirlooms and Accessories (triptych), 2002 ink-jet prints on paper in wooden artist's frames with rhinestones 51 x 46 inches.

© Kerry James Marshall Courtesy of the artist and Jack Shainman Gallery, New York.

If you choose to sit with the image, rather than bypassing the painful truth of it, remarkable insights can take place. You may notice a few things such as the following:

Parts

- ◆ Three women who appear white bodied are facing the camera.
- ◆ The faces of these women are framed in a necklace.
- ◆ Their throats are visible.
- ◆ A triptych format.
- ◆ A necklace that looks like pearls.
- ◆ A chain link necklace.
- ◆ A fishbone necklace.
- ◆ The frames are white.
- ◆ The image of the lynching is etched faintly.
- ◆ One necklace is broken.
- ◆ Two necklaces are composed off the frame.
- ◆ White space overlays the image of the lynching.

If we take a moment to consider a few possible purposes of each part we listed, we might make the following connections or inferences:

Purposes

- ◆ *A part: Three white bodied women are facing the camera.*
  - o Purpose: To show three generations of white bodied women as accessories to the brutal lynching of Black bodied men.
- ◆ *A part: The faces of these women are framed in necklaces.*
  - o Purpose: To expose the way white bodied women have been portrayed as precious objects immune from complicity in murder.

    o   Purpose: The women are depicted as white female cameos, also in ropes and chains.
◆ *A part: A triptych format.*
    o   Purpose: To hold the image of three white bodied women as separate individuals, but also in connection with each other.
◆ *A part: A necklace that looks like pearls.*
    o   Purpose: Could this denote class status amongst the three women?
◆ *A part: A chain link necklace.*
    o   Purpose: It is the same shape of chains used to enslave Black people.
◆ *A part: A fishbone necklace.*
    o   Purpose: Does this signify the "easy pickings" of fish in a barrel?
◆ *A part: The frames are white.*
    o   Purpose: The structure of our society is framed by white bodied immunity.
◆ *A part: The image of the lynching is etched faintly.*
    o   Purpose: Our gaze is turned to the white bodied audience to witness the brutality in their casualness.
    o   Purpose: The white bodied women seem protected by all the white color that surrounds them.
◆ *A part: One necklace is broken.*
    o   Purpose: Who broke the chain?
    o   Purpose: To expose what has been broken. To expose implied immunity.
◆ *A part: Two necklaces are composed slightly off the frame.*
    o   Purpose: What parts of our heirlooms do we not make visible?
◆ *A part: White space overlays the image of the lynching.*
    o   Purpose: Whitewashing of a U.S. history of brutality against Black bodies.
    o   Purpose: Everyone here is caught up in a deadly frame of whiteness.

Complexities

◆ A complexity: How important it is to face this image, particularly for white identified educators. United States data reported in 2022, that 79.9 percent of teachers were white bodied, 76.8 percent are women, 6.1 percent were Black bodied, 9.4 percent are Hispanic/Latinx, 2.4 percent are Asian, 1.6 percent identify as two or more races, 0.4 percent are American Indian or Alaskan Native, 0.2 percent are Native Hawaiian or Pacific Islander. These numbers do not match our national student demographics. What these numbers reflect is a predominantly female, white bodied led school educational landscape (Taie & Lewis, 2022). This poses direct consequences for our children and our nation. There is a direct correlation between this particular past and our contemporary forms of education. Statistically, Black boys are more likely to be placed in special education classes. Black girls face a rate of expulsion that far exceeds white counterparts. Will our Black bodied students ever have a liberatory experience in education if teachers carry out lineages connected to devastating brutality? Will children of the global majority continue to be taught through a dominant caste lens? What is the cost to our future if we don't acknowledge what has happened, tend to our collective grief, and move through it?

◆ A complexity: Trauma. Most humans have experienced trauma of some kind. It can be hard to acknowledge systemic traumas and hold our shared histories when we ourselves are moving through personal pain, our own childhood adverse effects, or have experienced the unimaginable. Sometimes we simply move through life a bit numb, but personal and social healing is available and possible. Focusing on our personal healing impacts the health of the community at large. This is a window of opportunity.

Thomas Shipp and Abram Smith

The young men who were lynched in the photo, Thomas Shipp and Abram Smith, both 19 years old, along with 16-year-old James Cameron were falsely accused by Mary Ball of a sexual assault crime. They were locked in the town jail in the middle of the night. On the morning of August 7, a large white mob used an assortment of weapons and tools to break into the jail. They beat and tortured the men and hung them from a nearby tree. James Cameron miraculously survived. Thomas and Abram did not. When their bodies were removed from the tree, the mob moved in and took pieces of their bodies as souvenirs, which was a common practice for the white lynch mobs of the time to do. Mary Ball later stated that the men were innocent.

This was not an isolated case of a white bodied woman making false claims. This is a pattern that was endemic throughout the United States, seen also in the infamous murder of the child Emmett Till. It is a pattern of behavior that has perpetuated itself when white bodied women have been seen in recent years calling police on Black bodied men for birdwatching in the park or for having a barbeque at a lake. Crimes were not committed in either of these recent cases. Both women deemed Black bodied, male identified people as dangerous and a threat when no threat was visible. In these cases, white bodied women embodied an heirloom stance of racialized hierarchy and superiority and used calling the police as a threat to wield caste power. Their racialized and biased responses were knowingly or unknowingly connected to beliefs and behaviors of the past. In the whitewashed background of these seemingly innocuous incidents looms the threat of prison and of death for the Black bodied men. It is not a far reach to see correlations of these heirloom responses echoed in contemporary incidents of excessive suspensions of Black bodied boys in public schools, which statistically start as early as in preschool.

As a white bodied educator early in my career, I made the mistake early on of over-empathizing with the struggles my predominantly Black bodied students faced. I had believed that in loving them, and because I had faced many of the same adverse childhood experiences some of my students had, it was appropriate for me to cry their tears with and even for them. I learned quickly that empathy is indeed not the same as solidarity, and that my external presentation as a white bodied female crying about systemic racism meant many of my students felt they had to go into an "appease" survival response. This meant they were unconsciously being asked to abandon their own experiences and feelings, and instead to take care of my emotions.

This was pointed out to me by a Black bodied female colleague back when I was under the early-aughts-well-intentioned-white-educator operating system of a "we-all-are-one" color-blindness ideal. This is perhaps a spiritual and scientific truth, but also an oversimplification that leads swiftly to bypassing and white-washing impacts of systemic racialized oppressions. As defensive as I felt and as uncomfortable as I got, and as unskillfully as I responded at the time to this important feedback, over time I continued to process and look back beyond my own personal story. There was a terrible lineage behind this unconscious narrative my students and I had played out as if scripted. Historically in the United States, a white female crying about a racialized experience could lead to violence, and at one time even death, often against a Black male body in the form of a lynching. At the same time, many of my students had learned from an early age that it was dangerous for them to express any emotion, from anger to sorrow, in a mixed racialized space.

It may seem like a giant leap from my intent of great empathy to the impact of harm, but our inherited and ingrained caste system is often so deep we don't know it is in operation. My emotional responses were yet another unchecked privilege. I had to come to both acknowledge and sublimate what I would go on to refer to as my own "whiteness in space" in order to decenter myself.

As a theater director, I could not always hold back tears at the beauty of the performances my students gave and the stories they created, played out, and told. It still takes some martial arts-like skills to keep my emotions in check so that they do not inadvertently take over the space, even when they are based in love. Nowadays when I feel the impulse to relate a little too hard, I try to keep Dr. Cornel West's words in mind, that "Justice is what love looks like in public."

– Jessa

What Heirlooms Do You Carry?

What have you inherited and what healing does it need going forward? Each of us has a legacy connected to somebody or something. We come from lineages we may love and adore or reject and feel repulsed by, or know very little about. We may come from chosen lines of artistry and expression and fixed lines we had no choice but to understand and make choices around. Some of us have beloved heirlooms that have been passed down, generation to generation, be they physical objects or intangible items such as a song or a recipe. Others may have little record of what came before, if we were forced to flee a home country, or experienced a natural disaster, or if we have suffered a disconnect with our families of origin.

This work of looking at our heirlooms challenges our past ideas and understanding of what we've been told about our positionality on the planet. This creative practice asks us to look at what we have inherited, physically but primarily metaphorically, from a historical perspective regardless of what bodies we are physically expressed in.

The experience of Heirlooms and Accessories was designed specifically to address the aforementioned imbalance of a majority white female educators in our schools that serve and love a range of ethnically and racially diverse student bodies. When experiencing the work in a mixed crowd, it is important to offer participants of the global majority a choice in participation. For those that would like to pursue the work, we invite a focus on where there has been joy, resistance, and love rather than focusing on the traumas that have befallen ancestral lineages. For white identified educators, we encourage a stretch into some discomfort within a range of tolerance, which may illuminate stuck patterns and release unproductive shame by association.

Heirlooms and Accessories

Locate an heirloom, real or imagined. If it is within your space of being, go get it and have it next to you for the following artistic research. This work is dedicated to our ancestors: past, present, and future. The legacy of enslavement and genocide require a process of truth and reconciliation. This work begins with ourselves and extends into our leadership and sacred space of teaching and learning.

Figure 18.2 Heirloom pearls.

This artistic research and engagement may stir some cellular level discomfort, wisdom, or awe. As we work with lineage and talk about heirlooms and accessories, remind yourself of the opportunity for specifically disrupting the ongoing harm of inequity and racism. As educators, just as it is essential to study and revisit our subject area for mastery, it is essential we investigate our own long held lineages and narratives and make them visible to ourselves, so that we may more consciously understand the perspectives we are bringing with us into our classrooms. Perspectives that serve us, our teaching and our students, we can celebrate and lean into. Perspectives that cause harm, we have the power to disrupt and heal. We cannot hope to hold socioemotionally connected learning spaces that are culturally responsive experiences for our students without embarking on this work ourselves.

For people of the global majority, this work is for us too. Being in a body that represents the global majority doesn't mean that we don't have our own work to do. It will look different and feel different for each person as our collective experiences of colonization have taken on a broad range of historical trauma and cultural impacts. Add to this the ongoing implications of a social system which requires further commodification of our bodies to this day, which elicits a journey that only you can take toward a path of embodied liberation.

We are also not so bold as to say that every person representing the people of the global majority needs to be on a path of embodied liberation, as you may already be light years ahead of the majority of us. Freedom takes forms that only we can claim and name for ourselves. With that, heirloom work is for us to determine what we would like to address, either to disrupt and heal something or generate more restorative things such as rest and joy. For example, if you are working on a joyful life experience, select an heirloom that will have stories to tell you about joy.

Remember to review and make use of the pathways of engagement. Directly addressing systemic racism can be charged with generational pain, but also generational healing for everyone involved. As complex humans, we contain many intersectional ethnic and cultural identities, and have many unique experiences leading to unique responses to intense imagery or engagement with our lineages.

Given how our experience of external and internal oppression plays out within a society built on a caste system, some common responses to such stressors have been identified. People of the global majority (Black, Brown, AAPI, Indigenous bodies) and white or light bodied people will often experience a diverse range of reactions and feelings. It is typical to experience a strong emotional reaction alongside ancestral artistic research, and when this happens, find your breath, take a walk, journal, dance it out, or play a comforting song. Then return to the process.

- ◆ Expect discomfort, especially when processing personal lineage in a professional environment. Notice and locate it in the body and/or breath.
- ◆ Expect relief: All mammals move and shake to release trauma. Try shaking out your hands or feet or respond as feels appropriate through physical movement or sound.
- ◆ Practice affirmations that encourage your growth. Affirm your own ability to bring healing to yourself and your lineages.
- ◆ Proceed in a consent-based way: Ancestral lineages can bring up a lot of unexpected information and emotions. Enter in a way that feels generative and healing, pause for self-care as needed.

For people who are white-or light-bodied, it is typical to gravitate toward any of the above and also to experience the following:

- ◆ Shame, which can lead to a fight, flight, freeze, appease, or annihilate response, otherwise known as an amygdala hijack.
- ◆ An urge to become the authority in the room, respond defensively, and/or cry.
- ◆ An urge to inappropriately attempt to protect or be a savior to other adults in the space.

These responses can be experienced by others as fragility, or even as threatening to well-being. It can also inadvertently recenter whiteness in space. Trust your ability to grow beyond these initial common reactions by pausing, observing, and listening deeply to those most directly impacted by experiences of racialized oppressions in your community of practice.

If you wish to learn more about what you hear, there are many resources available online and from other white-bodied allies in undoing racialized harms. Resmaa Menakem in particular has done compelling work on the embodiment of racialized stressors as held by diverse bodies (2021).

For white and light bodied folks, it is almost never appropriate to ask our colleagues of the global majority to educate us further on experiences of racism, which can inadvertently further the harm and othering already experienced. It also places an undue burden on folks of the global majority to educate while also healing. White and light bodied folks who have inherited the U.S. caste system—not created it, but benefited from it nonetheless—have the majority of work to do when it comes to transforming caste based inequities in education and beyond. At the same time, if a colleague of the global majority offers the gift of discussing a racialized experience, take note.

Playwriting

Prepare yourself to do some playwriting. Playwrights such as the great August Wilson have used ancestry, lineage, and cultural objects of great importance to spark creative masterpieces and help us to form a deepened relationship to the past in ways that would otherwise remain unknowable.

Return to your heirloom, real or imagined. Observe your heirloom. Hold it in your hands if you are able to. Use all of your senses to consider it closely. Notice its weight, size, shape, texture, smell, taste, and so forth. Use your imagination to anthropomorphize your heirloom, imbuing it with a personality and life of its own.

Ask the heirloom
◆ Who do you come by way of?
◆ Before that?
◆ What have you witnessed?
◆ What have you heard?
◆ Whose hands have held you?
◆ What else have those hands held?
◆ Whose eyes have beheld you?
◆ What else have those eyes beheld?

Now with your journal in front of you, take a moment to write a story through the voice of this heirloom. Bring your heirloom to life by writing a paragraph or page-long monologue that encapsulates what you noted from the foregoing inquiry process.

What Were You an Accessory To?

This next part of our artistic research extends into working with an imagined or real ancestor related to the heirloom. Activate them through your mind's eye and imagine them going about their daily lives in relation to the object. Imagine yourself in their world, as though you are sitting together in their environment. Notice any details about this environment, such as the temperature, time of day, and specific location. Imagine looking into their eyes and ask them the following questions:

Ask the ancestor:
◆ What were you an accessory to?
◆ What inheritance have you left me?
◆ What healing do you need?

Repeat these questions until you can imagine a response coming through. Write down any words, phrases, songs, images, ideas, or information that came through this part of the work.

To complete this process, return to your heirloom monologue and read it side by side with your notes from your artistic research on an ancestor. To advance the work, do a rewrite that alternates or combines words and sentences from each section of your work. Create a dialogue between your heirloom and your ancestor. If you feel compelled to add your own voice or perspective as a third character, you are invited to do so. This may end up taking the form of a short play, or a poem. There is not a wrong way to engage this creative practice. If you are moved to read this aloud, or share with others, we invite you likewise to do so. It can be incredibly powerful to share artistic research of this depth with others. You might also choose to let it rest in your journal or turn it into a piece of artwork that can alter/altar your creative learning space.

> Those soft wrinkled hands that toil...snappin' beans.
> I am a storyline that is evolving.
> Sunday dinners.
> From earth to forest
> What heirlooms do you carry?
> Hang the clothes and wash the dishes.
> What healing do you need?
> Labored walks in stone fruit fields.
> You gave me a set of instructions. A social pattern time to shed,
> a storyline cast in the likeness of a summer storm.
>
> Compiled poetry responses

Figure 18.3 Combined heirlooms poetry.

Towards a Liberatory Educator Stance

We cannot boldly take a liberatory educational stance without having practiced the undoing of our own heirlooms and accessories tied to past personal and systemic harms. What things must change in our teaching practice as we review our artistic practice? What is important enough to help preserve and what aspects will remain the same?

We will caution that it can feel unnerving when we return to our teaching spaces after actively engaging in artistic explorations of race and caste. It can lead to a dissonance we weren't expecting. We might view a poster on our wall and now have the awareness to take it down immediately, or we might take note that we have been inadvertently calling more often on white bodied students in class or allowing a certain group to dominate class decisions. We may realize we have to relinquish unearned power we have held, or advocate for new forms of leadership at our school sites. We might have to give up singing a beloved childhood song or book we love to teach that we now realize has harmful lyrics or stereotypical portrayals. When this happens in real time, don't be afraid to say "pause" or "rewind" or "hold, please." Give yourself a second, or a minute, or a day, or a year to ground, reframe, and determine actions you need to take, words you need to clarify or state, and changes that might need to occur. We're on this liberatory path together to reach a more full experience of ourselves, which in turn avails us to facilitate a more full experience for our students.

A Letter to Her Teachers

As a black person that goes to this school I feel out of place.
When I walk into a classroom I see no one that looks like me,
no one whose hair is like mine, no one whose skin is as dark as mine.
I see a teacher that subconsciously thinks less of me because of the color of my skin.
I feel like I have to do twice as much as the other kids just to get where they started.
It's hard to walk around with what the world sees as the face of crime,
with the face of aggression, with the face of not being educated.
It's not only my skin but my hair as well.
Wherever I go I get told that my hair isn't correct.
I'm scared to wear it down because I don't know what someone's going to put in it.
That thought is a thought no white girl will ever have to carry around
and a thought no girl should have to carry around.
When I point out people's microaggressions
they make me the mad guy,
the guy that makes everything about race.
As a black person I can't look at the world the same way as a white person.
So I always have the thought "was it because I'm black?" in the back of my mind.

A teacher once gave me every reason why I shouldn't feel that way
and the way I look at the world is wrong.
In math, some kid tried to stick a ruler into my hair.
I raised my voice at him and told him how that was racist,
I was the one who got a talking to by the teacher about raising my
voice.
The teachers look at the reaction from the black student
and not what they are reacting to
because when black people get loud
they think more of it
because the world has told us that black people are aggressive
and that we should be feared.
by Jayla Sherman, Middle School Student, 2023

Creative Inquiries
What have I learned from exploring the lineage of harmful norms
and established systems of oppression through the visual arts and
playwriting?
How can I implement the use of creative and imaginative dialogue in
my classroom for introspection, identification, understanding, and
building an artful and culturally responsive learning experience?

Bibliography

Marshall, Kerry James. (2017, August 31). Heirlooms & Accessories, 2002. The
Studio Museum in Harlem. https://studiomuseum.org/collection-item/
heirlooms-accessories

Menakem, R. (2021). *My Grandmother's Hands: Racialized Trauma and the Pathway
to Mending Our Hearts and Bodies.* Penguin Books.

Taie & Lewis. (2022). *Black or African American Teachers: Background and School
Settings in 2017–18.* https://nces.ed.gov/pubsearch/pubsinfo.asp?pubid=
2022024

19

Queering the Curriculum

Beyond the Confines of a Social Structure

One of my mentors and teachers has been the renowned dancer and choreographer Anne Bluethenthal. She shared the idea of queering the curriculum with me over a decade ago, as a dancer and educator in the San Francisco Bay Area. In Anne's work, the work of queering means to break with an ordinary paradigm and create new language through movement. It means moving outside of the structures and disciplines we are asked and often told to live within. Queering the curriculum is a liberatory action that leads to learning spaces beyond inclusion and into belonging.

As a student of Anne's in the first MFA class in Interdisciplinary Studies and Creative Inquiry at the California Institute for Integral Studies, I was introduced to her concept of queering as not only an identity but as a methodology for creative process. Anne's company ABD Productions produces the ensemble Skywatchers, a relational performance ensemble that centers formerly unhoused folks in the Tenderloin District of San Francisco.

As a queer-identified artist, Anne embodies the notion of queering in her own choreography and staging as a sociopolitical creative act. Her version of queering is to express movement not only by pushing up against dominant cultural narratives but by quite literally shifting a gesture. For example, if a physical task or action is "to knock on the door" or to "dance a waltz," she might invite an exploration to "queer" the gesture, or to shift the pace, direction, range, shape, or

DOI: 10.4324/9781003301226-23

quality of a movement. In rehearsal or performance, this might end up looking like using a knee to knock on a door in slow motion, or perhaps a same-gender couple waltzing forehead to forehead. Queering allows the performer to abstract the conventional to express something beyond the expected norm, and for an audience to experience something familiar in a divergent way. For Anne, queering often looks like applying divergent and convergent creative thought as a gesture or action, a stance that aligns well with her social justice ethos and actions as an activist in the world.

– Jessa

The notion of queering the curriculum helps us to locate the profound sense of freedom we wish for ourselves and our students to experience in the world. Freedom can be found for many in the social body of queerness. The orientation of queerness is not only a sexual orientation, but also often living in a way unbothered by restrictions of religion, culture, politics, and the gamut of ideologies that remain in place for purposes of power, domination, and control. It is a confrontation with outdated models of culture and what it means to "be allowed" to be a human being.

> The workshop asked us to think of a problem or issue that impacts queer students & staff. Then we were asked to "queer up the problem." I had a lot of trouble understanding how to do this because to me, "If we queered up the problem, the problem wouldn't exist." And that ultimately led me to realize, "In fact, if we queered up most of our societal problems or issues, they wouldn't exist either."
>
> – Maya Kosover, Teacher & Artist

Queering the curriculum is the continuation of lesson design that loves your students as you strip away remaining barriers that may limit someone's personhood. It is the expansion of liberated teaching and learning that removes any homophobic, patriarchal, binary, one dimensional, or limited gender and sexuality–based narratives found in dominant culture.

Creative Inquiries for Educators Identified as LGTBQIA+
  Who are the people who have loved you into existence?
  Where do you experience the most joy and freedom?
  What creativity is found in your own experience of liberation?
  How does that translate to your students?
  How do we "queer the curriculum" on behalf of our students and
    ourselves?

Figure 19.1 Queering the curriculum art piece.

Dissonance

If you're experiencing cognitive or cultural dissonance as an educator, we invite you to take that on as artistic research. People who may have few remaining racialized or colorist biases may still assign stereotypical qualities or negative judgements to those who identify as queer, gay, lesbian, bisexual or outside of a heterosexual identity in any form. Our cultural lineages may be a source of limitation or liberation when it comes to expectations around gender roles. As with racialized discrimination, gender-based violence, especially against those in the transgender or gender nonconforming community, leads to a mortality rate that is significantly higher when compared to cis gendered men or women. Continue to use the tools we've described so far to think through and explore why you might be stuck.

Creative Inquiries for Educators Not Identified as LGTBQIA+
    Is your framing of the world resonating or jarring with the topics at hand?
        Why is that?
    Are you being asked to let go of old patterns of beliefs and thoughts?
    Are you growing beyond a particular lens on the world?
    How might our lessons and pedagogical stances reflect our students better?
    How do we "queer the curriculum" on behalf of our students and their
        their families?

When we grow beyond our mind's current frames, often reach what many like to call cognitive dissonance. Dissonance feels like reaching a junction point along a path and not being sure which way to move forward. Claiming cognitive dissonance is theoretically an appropriate response. It is your mind saying "Hey, I wasn't built with these narratives, they don't make sense to me." When we introduce a new idea or way of thinking (and being) that clashes with what we've been told by our cultures or lineages, there is dissonance. But dissonance doesn't mean we stay stuck. It means we select which way we're going to keep moving. And we keep moving in the direction that opens versus the direction that narrows.

At this time, depending on our location within a particular community or global context, youth are often freer to directly express gender and sexual identities, and yet this liberation continues to be a matter of life and death for all too many. Take a moment to consider the following statistics of LQBTQIA+ youth and your own experiences. In what ways do society's perceptions, understandings, and ideas need to evolve in order for these statistics to change?

- *40 percent of LGBTQIA+ youth* respondents have considered suicide
- *29 percent of LGBTQIA+ youth* have experienced homelessness
- *1 in 3 LGBTQIA+ youth* reported that they had been physically threatened or harmed
- *Transgender and nonbinary youth* whose pronouns are respected attempted suicide at half the rate of those whose pronouns weren't respected

(Trevor Project, 2020)

Select *one* of the data points above to consider and journal to or ideally discuss with a colleague (either at this time or in another moment if you are working independently.)

Creative Inquiries

What stands out to you with this data?

What connections are there between this data, your self, and your own students?

For educators who identify as LGTBQIA+, how has your identity and positionality been of service to your teaching practice?

For educators who are not personally LQBTQIA+ identified, are there blind spots or patterns in your teaching and learning or curricular narrative that have perpetuated othering of LGBTQIA+ students or families that are LGTBQIA+ identified?

Given the data at hand, how can your lessons respectfully love and serve your students regardless of their gender or sexual identities, some that may still be forming?

Choreography

We are going to invite you to do a bit of writing and then practice some movement, or choreography. If you are working in a group setting, gather in small groups or as partners. Take no more than a few minutes for each person. If you are sharing, the goal is to share without interruption. Share your responses to each question without a dialogue with your partner or partners. If you are listening, the goal is to listen without interruption. Hold a space for listening with love and respect.

1. Power as creative inquiry:
   a. Share any of your foregoing creative inquiry responses that you would like to discuss with your partner.
   b. What educational power dynamics are you now reckoning with, risking, queering, or disrupting and how?
2. Select or write down three short phrases from your responses that you would like to work with.
   a. Speak these three phrases out loud as a text or dialogue, for example you might say...
      i. "Standards are the rule of law"
      ii. "Artistry is the way forward"
      iii. "Students are beyond standard"
3. Take a moment to stretch the body before we move on. Find a way to engage in physical movement that is accessible to you. Now considering your responses, we are going to create a piece

of choreography. Add three compelling, metaphorical, or abstract gestures in order to create a beginning, middle, and an end. Repeat the gestures and the phrases until they are in your muscle memory.

4. Now, let's use Anne Bluethenthal's frame here and "queer" the movement in some way—perhaps you want to take a risk and do the movement backward, faster, slower, or add rhythm or sound. Explore your entire range of motion, explore repetition, echo, and qualities of weight and flow. Play with a range of emotional states, facial expressions, movement, and sound until there is a new discovery that feels like a breakthrough for you. You can let go of the original language if you wish, or maybe it becomes a song or a breath. Now title this choreography "Queering the Curriculum."

5. Take a moment to reflect in your journal on everything that showed up for you. How is this choreography in relationship with the creative inquiries you explored earlier? What meaning does this choreography signify for you? Does it bring you joy, does it feel strong? Does it contain sorrow or a call to action? If you wish to expand your artistry here by combining the earlier journal or discussion points, or even by adding a musical score or costume and makeup to this movement, please do so.

As we commit to lessons that love our students, it is essential that we demonstrate safe environments for full expression of gender and sexual identity, as has long been available to so many in and through the arts. The ability to put on a mask and perform an authentic version of selfhood in joyous and life-affirming ways can perhaps be made most visible through the artistry of drag performers, popularized by such cultural phenomena as *RuPaul's Drag Race*.

Theater in particular has long provided a safe haven for marginalized individuals to have their stories not only acknowledged but very literally applauded. LGTBQIA+ and otherwise nonconforming youth have quite literally had their lives saved by entering this location as a place of belonging. Many of us who take pride in being self-proclaimed "theater geeks" may also identify with a shared queerness in the theater that holds a long cross-cultural tradition of exploration and acceptance of diverse gender expressions and sexual identities.

Many of my students over the years have used the opportunity for gender-fluid casting to explore their own gender identity and even to come out as gender-queer, gay, bisexual, lesbian, nonbinary, or trans to their friends and family. By first acknowledging themselves within the safer context of a play or a performance, they were then able to step into lives of authenticity and belonging and even beauty in the "real" world.

– Jessa

Queering the curriculum means that we are actively creating spaces of belonging that eliminate constructions of gender and sexuality norms as patterned from heteronormative value sets. We are co-constructing a society that honors a gender expression and human attraction spectrum so that all beings can freely express and prioritize a life experience of their identity and choosing.

Critical Reflections
  In what ways might I invoke the provocation and understanding of how and why it's important to queer the curriculum? What is my role in queering the curriculum?
  Is my classroom creating a safe space of increased inclusion for all my learners, one that honors diverse gender expression and a spectrum of expressed and unexpressed sexual or relational preferences?
  Can I more often employ elements of dance and movement, music and media making, cartooning and graphic art as joyful processes with which to navigate a love-based classroom experience, especially in times of trauma or hardship?

Bibliography

ABD/Skywatchers. (n.d.). Abdproductions.org. https://www.abdproductions.org/

The Trevor Project. (2020). *2022 National Survey on LGBTQ Youth Mental Health*. Thetrevorproject.org. https://www.thetrevorproject.org/survey-2022/assets/static/trevor01_2022survey_final.pdf

20

From Implicit Bias to Explicit Belonging

Reshaping Thinking to Create Cultures of Care

Four children sat quietly around a table. They all had their *Explode the Code* books open and were collaborating on the work. They would consistently ask one child in particular, Quinn, if an answer was correct or not. This student was a blond haired, blue-eyed child whose parents dressed them in organic cotton clothes. Another student of the four, Angel, was a mixed-raced child from a large family. After making several observations of this ongoing behavior, I finally asked what I had already confirmed for myself. I asked the class one day, "Why does everyone ask Quinn for the answers?" And without any hesitation, the class fired back, because they are the smartest one. What I knew to be true was that Angel was actually the child in the class who was reading at a 4th grade level, and was quick to acquire the learning content. Their writing was imaginative and fun. They excelled in math as well. Angel was a critical thinker for a five year old.

I knew why my class thought Quinn was the smartest in the classroom. They were white and able-bodied, wore brand new shoes, followed the rules, were agreeable, and kind. Angel was a free thinker, enjoyed being in their own head, and they didn't share eagerly in our circle time like Quinn did.

That day, I introduced a new classroom job: Thought Partner. It meant that if a student had a question they couldn't figure out, they asked the thought partner before they asked me. Angel was named as

DOI: 10.4324/9781003301226-24

the first person to have this job. The interruption was successful. Students got to see how smart Angel was, and how smart everyone was!

What I learned was that we can make loving interventions to the biases that form in childhood, and we can make them early. Had I not recognized that my students were participating in patterns of perception and building bias in their brains, I could have easily not seen an issue and let my students continue to engage in their decided thinking, or judgments, about each other. It's never too soon to intervene.

– Mariah

How do we artfully disrupt bias to create cultures of explicit belonging and beloved community? Finding solutions to implicit bias like the foregoing example show that we are capable of designing for equity and belonging. To do so, we need to understand the complex role of bias in our thinking and behaviors toward others; then we are able to identify bias as it plays out in front of us.

Our aim as educators in understanding implicit bias is to acknowledge that the systems we've discussed thus far do exist, and that we can identify and understand how we've been operating within them, and trust that we are more than capable of evolving our personhood to repair and move forward. With vast information now available to us about how bias shapes our thinking and actions, we can take the time to explore its impacts and build toward repair through actions that increase belonging.

The Construction of Implicit Bias

The brain is a prediction making machine. It is a pattern making machine. It likes confirmation, and it likes to be right. Recall the work of breaking patterns. What still lingers from your artistic work to identify, understand, and create new patterns? Have you noticed an ability to identify more patterns as you've moved through this book? Patterns shape a wide range of what we know and reinforce ideas and behaviors. We encourage you to engage with this arc of learning as a flexible and iterative process. There can be great insight found in repeating praxis.

The prefrontal cortex is where our brains hold the awareness of considering our own thoughts with the ability to question. Research is constantly evolving, particularly in neuroscience, but what we know currently is that our brain functions with only 1 percent of *conscious* awareness—not to be confused with myths like "we only use 10 percent of our brain." We use our whole brain, but the amount of information that we are consciously aware of is a very small percentage of all that takes place. It's estimated that we take in about 11 million bits of information into our brains every second. However, our conscious minds can handle only 40 to 50 bits (Banaji & Greenwald, 2013). In order to handle all the incoming information, our brains have made shortcuts to process and store information.

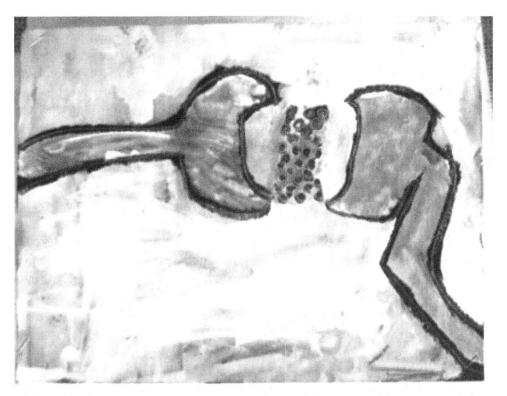

Figure 20.1 Student-made neuron art.

Cognitive bias is the natural outcome of our brain making a shortcut in order to manage information. These shortcuts, as understood by researchers studying implicit biases, are errors in how we read the world, encode the world, remember information, and engage in the world (Banaji & Greenwald, 2013). These errors are so ingrained that they are unconscious in us. Much like when our ancestors translated their world into a few lines on a cave wall, we still translate only a few elements of what actually exists in the world around us through our limited perception.

These inherent errors of perception are, in a way, attempting to make it easier for us to navigate the world. The problem is, depending on one's culture and caste structure, we have errors of thought or cognitive biases shaped by preexisting ideas that associate certain skin colors or facial features or other identity markers like gender with degrees of competency.

The caste system has been well grooved in our brains. This is where it is helpful to acknowledge how our brains have been molded unconsciously from the earliest ages to participate in the operating matrix of its design.

Our goal with understanding implicit bias is to acknowledge that these systems exist, how we've been operating within them, and to evolve our brain's capacity to move beyond these blindspots, mindbugs, perceptions, stereotypes, and racial disparities and into an expansive place where we live our lives free from limiting and oppressive behaviors, patterns, structures, procedures, and systems. What caste-based systems in your own life have been in place so long, they just look like the natural order of things?

The media has affected a lot of our behaviors and shaped a lot of our biases, and continues to do the same in the lives of our students. Data tells us that behind-the-scenes roles in Hollywood, such as producers, directors, writers, directors of photography, and editors, were 75 percent male and 25 percent female in 2021 (Lauzen, 2022). Each of these roles in Hollywood are also still overwhelmingly held by white bodied, cis gendered men. Because of this, a very limited gender, race, and caste perspective has had the power to shape our collective dominant cultural narratives. These narratives get hardwired into all of our brains, maintaining internalized social constructs.

Knowing that external systems can move slowly, how might we begin to evolve our own brains' capacity to confront and move beyond biases that cause harm, especially when that bias shows up in the classroom?

Do you notice how ideas return to you, how you grow and evolve from one state of thinking to another? This is the activation of a "return" which is found in the shape of a spiral. The spiral can help us understand the returning nature and development of the world around us.

A Pathway Forward

- Pause.
- Acknowledge that patterns of bias exist; understand their design and structure.
- Work at breaking through patterns of bias through a process of inquiry.
- Allow informed intentions, not biases, to guide action.

- Create supportive policies and procedures to disrupt bias and practice with consistency.
- When confronting your own biases in real time, perhaps take a moment to doodle a few spirals and consider how you might artfully reckon with them. The SPIRAL framework can support an iterative path of learning.
- Return to the Core Four to assess how power, narrative, lineage, and embodiment might be playing a role in this bias, and how they may also be used to help our conscious awareness to grow.

The practices that we have introduced along the way all support the work of building a community of care and advance equity and belonging. The praxis work situated in the arts and creative process supports the mind's expansion of the world around us. The work of *conocimiento* invites us to understand and know the world beyond our brain-bound thinking. Cultural and contemporary arts practices, both visual and performance, allow the mind to make meaning of a complex universe.

Our final artistic research practice creates an artful space between implicit bias and thoughtful response. The practice allows for observation and critical thinking to enter.

Verbatim Theater

Verbatim theater, or documentary theater, is a tool for creating empathy and social change by sharing narratives drawn from artistic research interviews. Verbatim theater is an excellent way to develop capacities for speaking and listening, to develop text and deepen understanding of multiple perspectives contained within any one story, community, event, topic, or truth.

Verbatim theater places the learner in a position of power by conducting "word-for-word" artistic research in the community and turning that research into performance. The practice of verbatim theater invites us to listen differently. It disrupts power and disrupts our internal monologues, which are generally going while others are speaking and can be filled with mindbugs! By listening to the exact words and phrases someone uses, rather than preparing our own opinions or responses to them, we are creating what implicit bias researcher Jennifer Eberhardt refers to as friction, or a pause between our patterned responses and inherent biases and our stories about what they mean. In this pause there is room for new information to be processed and assumptions to be repaired (Eberhardt, 2019).

Part One: The Gift of Being Seen and Heard

Figure 20.2 Students in verbatim performance.

Actress, playwright and professor Anna Deavere Smith is credited with the creation of verbatim theatre, or docu-drama, where she applies a unique approach to artistic research. The artistic research process involved in developing verbatim theater requires listening to a narrator tell a first-person story and perceiving a range of observable data as they do, much like a social scientist might. In this case, the data can include the narrator's gestures, tone of voice, facial expressions, linguistic patterns, rhythms of speech, body language, unique clothing or hairstyle markers, and sometimes "props" or objects. The verbatim theater artist does this in order to eventually accurately portray this narrator as a character and to express the narrator's lived truths and perspectives to the best of their ability.

Artistic Research for Verbatim Theater

It is easiest to begin this process by partnering with one other person and taking turns in the roles of artistic researcher and narrator. As your partner shares their story, take note of some but not all of the exact words and phrases being used. Jot them down as word-for-word as you can, or verbatim. Notice the aesthetic elements listed previously, and take note of anything specific you'd like to remember for resharing this story *as the narrator* later on. For example, note taking on gestures might look like this: "blinks eyes & looks to the left with pause in storytelling" or "emphasis on word NEVER, hand hits table".

◆ We are going to hold interviews that, in this case, call upon a piece of art from childhood. This could be a TV show you used to love, a favorite song, a play you saw, or a painting that hung at your grandma's house.
  ○ If you are working individually, we invite you to talk or video chat with someone you know well. If you are in a learning group, we invite you to pair up. Always ask for consent and share the intention of this artistic research process.
  ○ If you are working with a partner, the artistic researcher will listen and write down exact words and phrases that you hear—not all, but those that seem to hold the most meaning for the speaker.
  ○ If you are on your own, you can also watch a YouTube video of an expert, artist, or public figure you admire and follow the same prompts with the recorded video.

At this phase of the process, think of yourself as an ethnographer, a scientific observer, rather than as an interpretive artist quite yet!

Please remember the idea that listening and reflecting is a gift and an act of love. We are listening in order to understand, connect, and convey this person's truth and story, not to judge it or bring our own biases to it in any way. Having been heard and listened to deeply is a great gift.

Part Two: Interviews

Referring back to the Core Four, map your interviews based on the following questions. Each question is intended to support both the artistic researcher and narrator in gaining clarity around how media and culture may have caused us to develop unconscious bias.

What is an art piece you recall loving as a child?

Lineage: What is the lineage of this art piece? What genre/what came before it?

Narrative: Whose stories were central? What larger narratives about culture did it support?

Embodiment: How was this art held by you as a sensory experience? What kind of emotions and sensations did it elicit (i.e., did you feel excited, empowered, thrilled, entertained, seen, nurtured)?

Power: Locate any power dynamics present in this art. Who was it made by? Who did it give power to? Was this art a disruption of dominant cultural power or a reinforcement of it, or more nuanced and complex?

Part Three: Creation of a Performance Piece

For the artistic researcher: Using your notes of any exact words, phrases, gestures, and details you witnessed, take a few moments to compose an artful monologue from your partner's story. This story is a gift you will share back to your partner. Using artistic license, you can explore making use of repetition, elongating a sigh, or making a gesture more pronounced. To stay respectful to the story that was shared, try not to reinvent any words or phrases. Your performance piece may feel more akin to a poem than a play, and is obviously never about mimicking or mocking your partner's share. Quite the opposite, it is a great act of empathy to be able to metaphorically take a walk in someone else's shoes. If your narrator has an accent that is distinct from your own, or either of you have a physical tick, for example, our task as an actor is not to replicate these qualities but instead to find how they resonate in our own bodies. It can feel respectful to alter our vocal pitch and inflection, for example, rather than attempt to speak in a dialect not our own. We might move our bodies with a similar tempo as our narrator but not necessarily replicate unconscious or involuntary gestures, if doing so might cause harm.

An Offering

Take turns sharing your work with one another and perhaps within your larger community. Metacognitively reflect on what it was like to listen and be listened to in this way, and what value was there in performing one another and in being performed in building toward a beloved community. Consider the context of the stories that were shared, and how these early grooves in the brain may have shaped decisions and identities, and biases, later in life. Thank your partner.

In a unit on Community, students selected and researched a community member using a verbatim interview process. As part of artistic research, we outlined each student's body, which they then designed and painted as though they were the person they studied. We had a classroom full of people on the walls: a beekeeper, a doctor, a librarian, a paleontologist, a gardener, a truck driver, and a zookeeper, just to name a few. On the day of their interviews they came dressed as their person and sat propped on a stool where we all sat in a circle. They took questions from their peers, and if I needed to pry a bit more, I would interject a few questions here and there. They also interacted with each other as their chosen community member throughout the day.

– Mariah

Creative Inquiries

Why as educators is it especially essential that we embark on a proposed path to disruption of implicit bias in our own minds and actions?

How does research from social psychologists Dr. Mahzarin R. Banaji and Dr. Jennifer Eberhardt on how bias and blindspots operate inform my current curricular practices?

How might my classroom or school culture actually shift if I play with building belonging through artistic research, dialogue, and deep listening in the learning environment in an ongoing and sustainable capacity?

Bibliography

Banaji, M. R., & Greenwald, A. G. (2013). *Blindspot: Hidden Biases of Good People*. Random House.

Eberhardt, J. (2019). *Biased: Uncovering the Hidden Prejudice that Shapes What We See, Think, and Do*. Penguin Books.

Lauzen, M. M. (2022). *The Celluloid Ceiling*. Deadline.com. https://deadline.com/wp-content/uploads/2023/01/Celluloid-Ceiling-Report-2022-SDSU.pdf

Wilkerson, I. (2020). *Caste: Origins of Our Discontents*. Random House.

Ximo, C. O. M. (Ed.). (2011). *Anna Deavere Smith*. Ject Press.

21

The Radiant Child
Surpassing Standardized Assessments

Someone once asked me what I saw in the students that I taught. I responded by saying that I saw the universe unfolding in each student. I have always looked for the radiance in each child, because I know that our atoms are made of the same elements that make stars shine. I know that each child holds radiance. Artist Jean Michel Basquiat was known as the Radiant Child. His family saw his abilities to think profoundly and express ideas through artistic means. His teachers didn't always see that. In fact, they discouraged him from becoming an artist.

One tragedy of standardized testing has been the anesthetic result of compliance-based "teach to the test" teaching and learning. I was horrified walking into my mom's second grade classroom two years after No Child Left Behind was embraced. Gone was her art filled vibrant classroom where students sat in table groups and creativity was a value. Gone was the radiance. In its place were anchor charts and students sitting in rows. It pained me to see it. "What happened?" I asked her. "This is what the district demands we do now." she said, and shrugged her shoulders.

– Mariah

We are fortunate to be working with many educational leaders who are insistent on prioritizing joy and creativity. There is ample evidence that the reign of a dimmed down education is over. Leaders from across sectors working on

DOI: 10.4324/9781003301226-25

future solutions for sustainable life on this planet are espousing the dire need for creative thought. Teachers aspiring to design and implement lessons that love their students are living in times where it's possible to craft meaningful units of instruction that center student inquiry. Administrators are stepping forward to reckon with systems and structures of racialized and socialized harm, and provide students the opportunity to think creatively and critically to increase cognition and experience joy in thinking and learning. In fact, it's what many progressive school leaders are now looking to support in the educational spaces they serve.

Can We Assess Creativity?

How might we assess and evaluate learning as we enter into an era that has finally begun to prioritize creativity as central to that process? This question is of great debate in the cognitive and neuroscience community.

Derek Fenner was a colleague of ours at Alameda County Office of Education. The three of us would frequently have pedagogy talks as we designed coursework for the schools we worked with. It is Derek who shared with us that the root word of "assessment" is *assidere*—to sit beside. His gift in this moment of sharing was an opening in how we could begin to rephrase the role of assessment in learning. Our stance is that creativity assessments should not try to replicate the old standards of assessment. To sit beside someone and observe, guide, and listen as they come to articulate their own growth and development is far more love based than a checklist or scale of creative thought or expression. If we can begin a gradual release, letting go of standardized assessment demands and seeing the learner as inherently creative, we can start to consider worthy measures of success, such as how the learner might approach a task or concept next time through application of greater degrees of divergent or convergent thinking.

Let the learner learn to assess their own work. Let them complete and create their own rubrics. Let them write artist statements as assessment. Let them give peer feedback through love notes. Let their caregivers see them shine as often as possible, through community art nights and public performances.

It's not important if you see your student as not having achieved or attained a level of creative thought in comparison to another child or set of learners. We are aiming to actually constantly assess even more closely, in order to understand our radiant learners for where they are, what might become an obstacle to learning and joy, and to do our best to remove that obstacle and to support them in getting to where they have the possibility of going. Ideally, as liberatory educators, assessments are primarily for us, a way to help us shape lessons that can love our students even more precisely.

What if we consider creativity an orientation rather than a destination in the same way that we understand the concept of liberation? We are inherently creative beings with the capacity to explore and stretch beyond what we think is possible.

The Many Ways Assessment Takes Form

Performance-based assessments are ways that a child can authentically show what they know in new and novel contexts. For example, if a child learns about color theory through paint, will they apply their color theory knowledge to a set design for the school play? Or if a child learns the base chemistry for soil, will they be able to create fertile conditions for the growth of a seed they saved from their apple at home? Can the child who learns about mycelium figure out how mushrooms might be used in their backyard for composting?

Performance-based assessment is often spoken about as an *authentic* form of formative and summative assessment. Something is authentic when it is not contrived from a scripted curriculum or repeated year after year without student input.

> I loved teaching a unit called Breads Around the World. When I finally understood the concept of authentic assessment, I asked my students how they would like to show off their knowledge about bread. It was they who came up with a cooking show, not me! Together we watched a handful of cooking videos and made a list of what made them "good." Students started to build comprehension around story structure for a cooking show, the components of a cooking show and the visual aesthetics that held their attention. These ideas became the categories for a rubric that they then used to self-assess.
>
> – Mariah

Assessment Through Discourse

Friend and colleague Todd Elkin was a part of an art exhibit curated by artist Brett Cook, which also included me, Chinaka Hodge and Evan Bissell. We each had an opportunity to use the museum space at the Yerba Buena Center for the Arts to display our pedagogical approaches. Todd's exhibit was centered around Assessment as Dialogue. He encouraged viewers to understand that assessment can look like an engaged conversation with a learner or group of learners in which you, as teacher, note-take the insights shared and offered about core ideas. A container is built for discussion and democratic participation. Socratic seminar is a form of assessment as dialogue. Assessment as dialogue can take the form of a question and answer panel after an arts performance, where students respond to questions from the audience. It can also look like a one-on one-conversation where you interview a student on ideas being taught in class. My part of the exhibit focused on Making Learning Visible from Project Zero. Teachers were invited into the space where I facilitated learning on the idea of "re" in education. We discussed ideas like "recenter, remix, recreate, redesign" and got to some rooted values on the changes we desired to lead for. The room was activated with our words, inquiries and images: making our learning visible to the viewers and ourselves.

– Mariah

Rubrics and Self-Assessment

Rubrics remain a steadfast way to support learners through a progression of understanding. What rubrics often lack, however, is appropriate categorization that is truthful but not dehumanizing. Using categories like 1, 2, 3, 4 and 5 are only as informative as the letter grades A–F. Adding descriptive words like "emerging, developing, growing, expanding, and evolving" are much more clearly articulated toward the process of learning (and can be easily translated back into letter grades as your current systems require). The Studio Habits of Mind and even state and National Core Arts Standards can also be repurposed as excellent cross-content area rubrics.

Thinking Routines

Most thinking routines can serve naturally as formative assessments. They provide real-time insights into what students are thinking and perceiving. You will be able to note where students are not making connections, which will give you more information about how your lessons are supporting connections overall. This is a great opportunity to reframe gaps in knowledge that you see and reteach concepts. The LOVE Protocol can be used as a summative and formative assessment. Try it out. See how far it can take your critical thought.

The Core Four as Assessment Frame

The Core Four—power, narrative, lineage, and embodiment—have been used flexibly by educators to evaluate learning spaces, design lessons, and assess for cultural responsiveness. As a creative educator, we imagine that you will find new and brilliant uses to use the Core Four frame. Here's one approach:

- Draw two lines on a paper to make four sections. Label each section with one of the concepts.
- Fill in each section with depictions of the Core Four. Use words, colors, symbols, or images for these representations.
- Structure questions around power, narrative, lineage, and embodiment that will support teachers and staff to investigate and think through how they show up in their teaching and leading.

Assessment as Ethnography

By using the approach of the ethnographer, teachers can build understanding of practices in culturally responsive teaching and learning through the arts that rely on inquiry-driven field notes rather than a rubric or survey. Field notes help us to observe, identify, describe, and make meaning of the culturally responsive and artful teaching and learning experiences at hand. Field notes are meant to be a flexible tool appropriate for many applications: as self-assessment for growth, as a form of evaluation, in communities of practice, for coaching purposes, and even for backward planning and lesson design.

Return to Radiance

In the art world, creativity concerns itself less with quantitative evaluation and more with processes of critical reflection. Frameworks from the field for creative response such as Liz Lerman's Critical Response Process and Assessment as Discourse draw out discussions on what someone has an embodied understanding of and what could use further practice or exploration. Meaningful creative assessment considers input directly from the creators' own values and wonderings about process, technique, and impact.

How will your students show radiance? Assessment should function to bring you and your students more shine, reflecting how you have both grown and illuminating a path to travel where you can continue learning and evolving. As you research and design creative assessment practices, consider the radiance. In a world that is fraught, don't be afraid to look for illumination.

Bibliography

Alameda County Office of Education Integrated Learning Specialists' Department. (2014). STTArts: USDOE grant. https://www2.ed.gov/programs/artsedmodel/2014/alameda.pdf

"Change the Story / Change the World: Episode 64—A Conversation with Liz Lerman—Change the Story /Change the World." (2023). Captivate. Fm. https://change-the-story-chan.captivate.fm/episode/episode-64-a-conversation-with-liz-lerman-ch-2

Yerba Buena Center for the Arts. (2019, May 22). *Home*. https://ybca.org

Epilogue

Epilogue

22

Epilogue

Nahuales and the Artist Within

We sat in a small circle in the backyard of a local artist in San Cristobál in 2017. Cultural anthropologist Alberto Vallejo Reyna, who lived and worked out of the town's museum, gathered a small group of cultural scholars to share his work and insights on Mayan history and belief systems. Reyna's young daughter translated from Spanish to English as he spoke. The backyard was a simple structure of a bit of earth, a few plants, cement walkways and colorful paper peace flags swinging gently in the air. I had my journal out with watercolors and colored pencils handy. Mid-way through the lecture, the well of tears in my eyes could not be held back any longer. The tears dropped to the page and mixed with the color on my journal as I wrote ethnographic notes: "Every human has a nahual—that is to say, a costume, a personality, a role in society. They say that the most common illness of our time is that people don't follow their nauhual. ... That is, that people don't develop their spirit. ... the Maya in Chiapas translate the word *nauhal* into Spanish, they translate it as 'the art.' And this means each one of us has an art that we have to develop."

– Mariah

Alberto's words spoke to core beliefs about the role of art in all of our lives. We all have an artist that dwells in us. Said another way, we all have a creative

DOI: 10.4324/9781003301226-27

spirit to develop. Our work as educators is to bring out the artfulness of our learners, and we can only do so by being creative beings ourselves. The world needs more of our creative spirit at play. Imagine a society that is driven and fueled by arts and culture, versus the limited social constructs we have found ourselves operating within. What if we weighted the creative inner lives of our youth as our main priority, and loved them into a brighter existence?

Figure 22.1 Bending flowers.

Bibliography

Vallejo Reyna, A. (2018). Resistance, Spirituality, and Self Actualization through Other Calendars and Other Geographies. https://www.cnsjournal.org/resistance-spirituality-and-self-actualization-through-other-calendars-and-other-geographies/?fbclid=IwAR1F2voMQLxljBQ4AccFAl4_y3UugMeo9lj8upPR3R658Wnjgmd90gLdKfE

Made in United States
North Haven, CT
28 September 2024

57927726R00102